Sovereignty Sermons *of* JONATHAN EDWARDS

Sovereignty Sermons *of* JONATHAN EDWARDS

HENDRICKSON PUBLISHERS

Sovereignty Sermons of Jonathan Edwards

P. O. Box 3473
Peabody, Massachusetts 01961-3473
www.hendrickson.com

ISBN 978-1-68307-047-4

Originally published by Hendrickson Publishers in *Sermons of Jonathan Edwards*.

Printed in the United States of America

First Printing — September 2017

Contents

Preface

Jonathan Edwards (1703–1758)

The kind of religion that God requires, and will accept, does not consist in weak, dull, and lifeless "wouldings"—those weak inclinations that lack convictions—that raise us but a little above indifference. God, in his word, greatly insists that we be in good earnest, fervent in spirit, and that our hearts be engaged vigorously in our religion: "Be fervent in spirit, serving the Lord" (Romans 12:11).

Jonathan Edwards, *A Treatise Concerning Religious Affections* (1746)

For most twenty-first century Americans, Jonathan Edwards is a murky figure from the distant past. Most will recognize that he was a preacher, a few might remember his connections with colonial New England. And some might even associate him with the Great Awakening, the first spiritual revival in North America.

In fact, Jonathan Edwards is considered one of this country's greatest theologians, a thinker and philosopher who had a prophetic grasp of the impact that Enlightenment thinking and scientific endeavor would have on Christian thought and experience.

His Times

Edwards was born just eighty-three years after the Mayflower found safe haven in Plymouth Harbor on the western side of Cape Cod Bay in Massachusetts. Fewer than half of the 102 passengers on that famous voyage were English Separatists—those who sought to purify the established Church of England, and for their efforts were persecuted and forced out of England. Known as Puritans, it was their faith and values that were codified in the Mayflower Compact, and ultimately became the foundation of New England civil code and the very fabric of society and life in New England.

For a moment, imagine the times. When Jonathan Edwards lived, the colonies in America were not united. In fact, they were separated by religion and politics and countries of origin. Each colony had its own distinct values and laws, its own immigrant populations, its own industry and commerce. New England was just that: New *England*. They were English people intent on creating a godly commonwealth in a new land—the sort of government and society unavailable to them in England.

When Edwards lived, the colonies were tethered to Europe, England mostly, and those ties were tested repeatedly. Sometimes those ties were tightly reined in by English troops and governors intent on maintaining control of the colonies and garnering as much revenue for the Crown as possible. In other periods, the colonies seemed to be left to their own devices, to set up their own government and make their own decisions.

In 1700, the European population in all the American colonies was two hundred and fifty thousand; ninety-one thousand of whom lived in New England. By 1775, the population of the colonies had increased to two and a half million. During Edwards' lifetime, the colonies experienced considerable growth with all its attendant pressures and difficulties, particularly in New England, where everything—its values, its laws, its very society—was defined and designed in the light of Puritan Christianity.

There it is again—that word *Puritan*. It is a distorted word today, having come to refer largely to sexual mores that should more honestly be credited to Victorians. Puritan values were about strong families, ethical and moral behavior, and a strong work ethic—and their laws codified the behaviors that were expected of a godly people. While the law can, at least for a time, influence behavior, it cannot guarantee that the hearts of the citizens are righteous. It was no different in New England.

The Massachusetts colony assumed that all settlers were or should be Christian. In fact, it insisted, prohibiting immigrants who were Roman

Catholic or otherwise outside the fold. At the beginning in particular, a good portion of the early settlers came to escape religious persecution. Their faith was vital and personal. After all, nominal faith is unimaginable in a persecuted church. But within the first one hundred years of the colony—by the time Edwards was ready to begin his ministry—the Puritans were no longer the persecuted church; instead they had become the established church, with all its attendant benefits, including power and the tax revenues collected to support the church. And in an established church, nominal faith becomes the norm.

Edwards faced a generation plump and happy with their flourishing businesses and relatively peaceful lives. It was a generation filled with spiritual apathy, materialism, and worldliness, whose spiritual life was far from the vibrant faith of the settlers who had sailed from England just two generations before. Confronting this spiritual apathy would become Edwards' life work.

His Early Life

Jonathan Edwards was born in East Windsor, Connecticut, the fifth of eleven children and the only son—the son and grandson of Congregational pastors. He was a great student, fluent in Hebrew, Greek and Latin by the age of thirteen. He was also gifted in natural science and scientific methodology, and in philosophy. He entered the Collegiate School of Connecticut (later Yale) in 1716 to continue his formal education, and graduated at the head of his class in 1720, then immediately began his divinity studies. He served for a short time as pastor of a Presbyterian church in New York City, then returned to Yale in 1724 to become a senior tutor.

In 1726, Edwards accepted a call from the Congregational church in Northampton, Massachusetts, to serve as assistant pastor to his grandfather, Solomon Stoddard. Stoddard was a highly regarded cleric, a man beloved by his congregants and respected by the Native Americans. Edwards would serve in this church for twenty-three years, long after the death of his grandfather in 1729.

His Family Life

In 1727, Jonathan Edwards married Sarah Pierrepont, a young woman he had met while he was a divinity student at Yale. Their marriage was remarkable by the standards of any age. Jonathan adored his wife Sarah, whom he called "my dear companion." Together, they created a loving home and thriving family, a safe haven where Edwards was able to study and work. Sarah complemented Jonathan; she was practical and socially adept, while he was distracted and intellectual. Theirs was a marriage filled with companionship, lively conversation, and joy. Edwards and Sarah were attentive and available to one another; they nourished one another, enjoyed one another, and valued one another.

Like everything he did, Edwards was intentional about his family life. Jonathan and Sarah had eleven children, who all lived to adulthood. Edwards made his family a priority, routinely spending the hour before dinner each night with the children. When he traveled out of town, Edwards would take one child with him. Often in the afternoon, Edwards and Sarah would set out on horseback where chores and responsibilities would not interrupt their conversation. They each recognized that their family and their relationship were worthy of the same attention given to study or work.

His Ministry

Jonathan Edwards is inseparably linked with the spiritual revival called Great Awakening, for it was under his preaching in Northampton, Massachusetts, that the Awakening came in 1734. Edwards had followed his grandfather Solomon Stoddard as pastor of the Congregational church in Northampton. Stoddard himself was a great revivalist, preaching five successive revivals, but by the time Jonathan took the pulpit in 1729, he discovered the people "very insensible of the things of religion"—their faith was dry and stale and impotent.

There is an irony of sorts in this story. One of the reasons for Stoddard's great popularity is he relaxed church membership requirements: rather than proof of conversion, he opened the sacraments to everyone except those living openly scandalous lives. This "open admission" effectively removed the necessity for an individual personal spiritual experience with Jesus Christ. This policy, although it could be argued as necessary for a society that defined itself only in Christian terms, ultimately served to lead people away from faith, not towards it.

Edwards, on the other hand, had an intimate understanding, both from personal experience and from his studies, that God was knowable, and that it was only in a personal relationship that true "religion" would be found. He began preaching, and while it took several years, by 1733 he began to see change. In 1734, he preached a series on justification by faith, and by the end of that year, the spark had been lit in Northampton.

Revival had been occurring already in New Jersey, through the work of Theodore Frelinghuysen and Gilbert Tennent, encouraging people out of their spiritual lethargy. The message of revival was this: "Outward morality is not enough for salvation. An inward change is necessary." This message is very familiar to the American Protestant ear today, but it was a fresh word to people who had depended on their morality, their outwards actions, their conformation to "Christian" behavior, to secure their place in God's Kingdom.

Revival grew in Northampton, rippling throughout the area and even into neighboring Connecticut. Edwards continued his preaching and God continued blessing. In 1740, the Awakening exploded through the work of Anglican George Whitefield, who arrived in Boston for his second visit to the colonies, this time a six-week evangelistic tour of New England. Edwards was at the center still, but Whitefield became the instrument of expansion, bringing about the most widespread revival that the colonies had ever experienced.

By 1750, the Awakening had receded from public prominence, but it was in this year that Edwards' position with the Northampton church was severed after twenty-three years. The reason? He wanted to change the policy of "open admission" to the sacraments, begun by his grandfather. Edwards' insistence that "only persons who had made a profession of faith could be admitted to the Lord's Supper" enraged his parishioners, and he was asked to leave.

After a few lean months of unemployment, Edwards found a remarkable new work, that of pastor to settlers and missionary to Indians in Stockbridge, a work begun by David Brainerd in the western frontier of Massachusetts. In 1757, he was chosen president of the College of New Jersey (Princeton), and subsequently relocated in order to begin his work, leaving Sarah behind to finish the packing in Stockbridge. A few months after arriving in his new post, a smallpox epidemic broke out, and Edwards chose to receive the new (and risky) inoculation against the disease. Shortly after, he died from complications from that vaccination, on March 22, 1758. His final words in a message to his beloved Sarah were:

> *Give my kindest love to my dear wife, and tell her that the uncommon union which has so long subsisted between us has been of such a nature as I trust is spiritual and therefore will continue forever.*

His Legacy

Though largely associated with the Great Awakening, Edwards leaves a legacy far outside the reach of this remarkable work of God's grace in America. It was Jonathan Edwards who wrestled with the new issues of scientific discovery, the Enlightenment, and the Age of Reason in light of Christian teaching and experience. It was Edwards who faced the emerging climate of humanistic rationalism over the teaching of a personal and loving God. It was Edwards who developed the uniquely American themes of a redeemer nation and a covenant people, a theme that echoes still today in the American mind. It was Edwards who tackled the problem of spiritual deadness by recognizing the necessity of a personal religious experience and by embracing the supernatural work of the Holy Spirit to awaken and illuminate the heart.

Edwards left a remarkable body of work. He recorded his observations of the Great Awakening in several works, including *A Faithful Narrative of the Surprising Work of God* (1736), in *Distinguishing Marks of a Work of the Spirit of God* (1741) and in *Some Thoughts Concerning the Present Revival of Religion in New England* (1742).

In 1746, he wrote his most famous book, *A Treatise Concerning Religious Affections*. In it he examines the importance of religious "affections" or those "passions that move the will to act," arguing persuasively that true religion resides in the heart, the home of affections, emotions, and inclinations. While in Stockbridge, Edwards completed *Freedom of the Will, and Nature of True Virtue*, and began his massive *History of the Work of Redemption*, which he never completed.

And, of course, Edwards left his sermons. "Sinners in the Hands of an Angry God" (included in *Revival Sermons of Jonathan Edwards*) is very likely his best remembered sermon, often used as an example of the Puritan obsession with eternal damnation and a wrathful God. True, it is a call to repentance, one made to an audience who harbored none of this century's distaste and doubts concerning the reality of God's final judgment. However, in fact, this sermon is atypical of Edwards' preaching. He spoke more often of God's love and the joys of the Christian life than of the fires of Hell.

Edwards' preaching reflected two of his core beliefs: first, God is the central focus of all religious experience—not humankind or reason or morality. As one writer observes, "Edwards' universe, like his theology, is relentlessly God-centered." And second: knowing God is not merely a rational knowledge—mental assent to particular beliefs—but also a sensible knowledge—experienced, sensed. As the taste of sweetness is distinct from the understanding of sweetness, so a Christian not only believes God is glorious, a Christian also senses the glory of God in his heart.

This collection is a fine sampling of Edwards' sermons during his time in Northampton and Stockbridge. Some are revival sermons, calling for repentance and amendment of life; some are pastoral, some instructional, and others written for specific occasions. But each one is a brilliant and personal invitation to know God both through our intellect and through our affections. These are sermons that challenge our minds, but also, and perhaps more importantly, compel us to open our hearts to the sweet love and joy available to us in our life in Christ.

> *I am bold in saying this, but I believe that no one is ever changed, either by doctrine, by hearing the Word, or by the preaching or teaching of another, unless the affections are moved by these things. No one ever seeks salvation, no one ever cries for wisdom, no one ever wrestles with God, no one ever kneels in prayer or flees from sin, with a heart that remains unaffected. In a word, there is never any great achievement by the things of religion without a heart deeply affected by those things.*
>
> —Jonathan Edwards, *A Treatise Concerning Religious Affections* (1746)

Advertisement to the Reader, Respecting the First Sermon

This note was published as a preface to "God Glorified in Man's Dependence," (which follows, on p. 3). The 28-year-old Jonathan Edwards preached that sermon as a Public Lecture in Boston on July 8, 1731. It was later published "at the desire of several ministers and others in Boston who heard it," becoming Edwards' first publication.

It was with no small difficulty that the author's youth and modesty were prevailed on to let him appear a preacher in our public lecture, and afterwards to give us a copy of his discourse, at the desire of diverse ministers and others who heard it. But as we quickly found him a workman that needs not to be ashamed before his brethren, our satisfaction was the greater to see him pitching upon so noble a subject, and treating it with so much strength and clearness, as the judicious reader will perceive in the following composure: a subject which secures to God his great design in the work of fallen man's redemption by the Lord Jesus Christ, which is evidently so laid out, as that the glory of the whole should return to him, the blessed ordainer, purchaser, and applier; a subject which enters deep into practical religion; without the belief of which, that must soon die in the hearts and lives of men.

For in proportion to the sense we have of our dependence on the sovereign God for all the good we want, will be our value for him, our trust in him, our fear to offend him, and our care to please him; as likewise our gratitude and love, our delight and praise, upon our sensible experience of his free benefits.

In short, it is the very soul of piety, to apprehend and own that all our springs are in him; the springs of our present grace and comfort, and of our future glory and blessedness; and that they all entirely flow through Christ, by the efficacious influence of the Holy Spirit. By these things saints live, and in all these things is the life of our spirits.

Such doctrines as these, which, by humbling the minds of men, prepare them for the exaltations of God, he has signally owned and prospered in the reformed world, and in our land especially, in the days of our forefathers; and we hope they will never grow unfashionable among us; for, we are well assured, if those which we call the doctrines of grace ever come to be contemned or disrelished, vital piety will proportionably languish and wear away; as these doctrines always sink in the esteem of men upon the decay of serious religion.

We cannot therefore but express our joy and thankfulness, that the great Head of the church is pleased still to raise up from among the children of his people, for the supply of his churches, those who assert and maintain these evangelical principles; and that our churches (notwithstanding all their degeneracies) have still a high value for such principles, and for those who publicly own and teach them.

And as we cannot but wish and pray that the college in the neighboring colony (as well as our own) may be a fruitful mother of many such sons as the author, by the blessing of Heaven on the care of their present worthy rector; so we heartily rejoice in the special favor of Providence in bestowing such a rich gift on the happy church of Northampton, which has for so many lusters of years flourished under the influence of such pious doctrines, taught them in the excellent ministry of their late venerable pastor, whose gift and spirit, we hope, will long live and shine in this, his grandson, to the end that they may abound yet more in all the lovely fruits of evangelical humility and thankfulness, to the glory of God.

To his blessing we commit them all, with this discourse, and every one that reads it; and are your servants in the gospel,

—T. PRINCE and W. COOPER, Boston, August 17, 1731

God Glorified in Man's Dependence

Preached on the Public Lecture in Boston, July 8, 1731. (See "Advertisement," p. 1.)

"That no flesh should glory in his presence. But of him are ye in Christ Jesus, who of God is made unto us wisdom, and righteousness, and sanctification, and redemption: that, according as it is written, 'He that glorieth, let him glory in the Lord.' "—1 Corinthians 1:29–31

Those Christians to whom the apostle directed this epistle dwelt in a part of the world where human wisdom was in great repute; as the apostle observes in the 22nd verse of this chapter, "The Greeks seek after wisdom." Corinth was not far from Athens, that had been for many ages the most famous seat of philosophy and learning in the world. The apostle therefore observes to them, how God by the gospel destroyed, and brought to naught, their wisdom. The learned Grecians, and their great philosophers, by all their wisdom did not know God, they were not able to find out the truth in divine things. But, after they had done their utmost to no effect, it pleased God at length to reveal himself by the gospel, which they accounted foolishness. He:

> chose the foolish things of the world to confound the wise, and the weak things of the world to confound the things which are mighty, and the base

things of the world, and things that are despised, yea, and things which are not, to bring to naught the things that are.

And the apostle informs them in the text why he thus did, "That no flesh should glory in his presence," etc. In which words may be observed:

1. What God aims at in the disposition of things in the affair of redemption, viz. that man should not glory in himself, but alone in God; "That no flesh should glory in his presence, that, according as it is written, 'He that glorieth, let him glory in the Lord.' "

2. How this end is attained in the work of redemption, viz. by that absolute and immediate dependence which men have upon God in that work, for all their good. Inasmuch as:

- *First, all the good that they have is in and through Christ; He is made unto us wisdom, righteousness, sanctification, and redemption.* All the good of the fallen and redeemed creature is concerned in these four things, and cannot be better distributed than into them; but Christ is each of them to us, and we have none of them any otherwise than in him. *He is made of God unto us wisdom*: in him are all the proper good and true excellency of the understanding. Wisdom was a thing that the Greeks admired; but Christ is the true light of the world; it is through him alone that true wisdom is imparted to the mind. It is in and by Christ that we have *righteousness*: it is by being in him that we are justified, have our sins pardoned, and are received as righteous into God's favor. It is by Christ that we have *sanctification*: we have in him true excellency of heart as well as of understanding; and he is made unto us inherent as well as imputed righteousness. It is by Christ that we have *redemption*, or the actual deliverance from all misery, and the bestowment of all happiness and glory. Thus we have all our good by Christ, who is God.
- *Secondly, another instance wherein our dependence on God for all our good appears, is this:* that it is God that has given us Christ, that we might have these benefits through him; he of God is made unto us wisdom, righteousness, etc.
- *Thirdly, it is of him that we are in Christ Jesus, and come to have an interest in him, and so do receive those blessings which he is made unto us.* It is God that gives us faith whereby we close with Christ.

So that in this verse is shown our dependence on each person in the Trinity for all our good. We are dependent on Christ the Son of God, as he is our wisdom, righteousness, sanctification, and redemption. We are dependent on the Father, who has given us Christ, and made him to be these things to us. We are dependent on the Holy Ghost, for it is *of him that we are in Christ Jesus*; it is the Spirit of God that gives faith in him, whereby we receive him, and close with him.

Doctrine

"God is glorified in the work of redemption in this, that there appears in it so absolute and universal a dependence of the redeemed on him." Here I propose to show, first, that there is an absolute and universal dependence of the redeemed on God for all their good. And, secondly, that God hereby is exalted and glorified in the work of redemption.

I. There is an absolute and universal dependence of the redeemed on God.

The nature and contrivance of our redemption is such, that the redeemed are in everything directly, immediately, and entirely dependent on God: they are dependent on him for all, and are dependent on him every way.

The several ways wherein the dependence of one being may be upon another for its good, and wherein the redeemed of Jesus Christ depend on God for all their good, are these: viz. that they have all their good of him, and that they have all through him, and that they have all in him: that he is the cause and original whence all their good comes, therein it is *of* him; and that he is the *medium* by which it is obtained and conveyed, therein they have it *through* him; and that he is the good itself given and conveyed, therein it is *in* him. Now those that are redeemed by Jesus Christ do, in all these respects, very directly and entirely depend on God for their all.

1. *The redeemed have all their good* of *God.* God is the great *author* of it. He is the *first* cause of it; and not only so, but he is the *only* proper cause. It is of God that we have our Redeemer. It is God that has provided a Savior for us. Jesus Christ is not only of God in his person, as he is the only-begotten Son of God, but he is from God, as we are concerned in him, and in his office of Mediator. He is the gift of God to us: God chose and anointed him, appointed him his work, and sent him into the world. And as it is God that *gives*, so it is God that *accepts* the Savior. He gives the purchaser, and he affords the thing purchased.

It is of God that Christ becomes ours, that we are brought to him, and are united to him. It is of God that we receive faith to close with him, that we may have an interest in him. Eph. 2:8. "For by grace ye are saved, through faith; and that not of yourselves, it is the gift of God." It is of God that we actually receive all the benefits that Christ has purchased. It is God that pardons and justifies, and delivers from going down to Hell; and into his favor the redeemed are received, when they are justified. So it is God that delivers from the dominion of sin, cleanses us from our filthiness, and changes us from our deformity. It is of God that the redeemed receive all their true excellency, wisdom, and holiness; and that two ways, viz. as the Holy Ghost by whom these things are immediately wrought is from God, proceeds from him, and is sent by him; and also as the Holy Ghost himself is God, by whose operation and indwelling the knowledge of God and divine things, a holy disposition and all grace, are conferred and upheld. And though means are made use of in conferring grace on men's souls, yet it is of God that we have these means of grace, and it is he that makes them effectual. It is of God that we have the Holy Scriptures; they are his word. It is of God that we have ordinances, and their efficacy depends on the immediate influence of his Spirit. The ministers of the gospel are sent of God, and all their sufficiency is of him. 2 Cor. 4:7: "We have this treasure in earthen vessels, that the excellency of the power may be of God, and not of us." Their success depends entirely and absolutely on the immediate blessing and influence of God.

First, the redeemed have all from the grace *of God.* It was of mere grace that God gave us his only-begotten Son. The grace is great in proportion to the excellency of what is given. The gift was infinitely precious, because it was of a person infinitely worthy, a person of infinite glory; and also because it was of a person infinitely near and dear to God. The grace is great in proportion to the benefit we have given us in him. The benefit is doubly infinite, in that in him we have deliverance from an infinite, because an eternal, misery, and do also receive eternal joy and glory. The grace in bestowing this gift is great in proportion to our unworthiness to whom it is given; instead of deserving such a gift, we merited infinitely ill of God's hands. The grace is great according to the manner of giving, or in proportion to the humiliation and expense of the method and means by which a way is made for our having the gift. He gave him to dwell amongst us; he gave him to us incarnate, or in our nature; and in the like though sinless infirmities. He gave him to us in a low and afflicted state; and not only so, but as slain, that he might be a feast for our souls.

The grace of God in bestowing this gift is most free. It was what God was under no obligation to bestow. He might have rejected fallen man, as he did the fallen angels. It was what we never did anything to merit; it was given while we were yet enemies, and before we had so much as repented. It was from the love of God who saw no excellency in us to attract it; and it was without expectation of ever being requited for it. And it is from mere grace that the benefits of Christ are applied to such and such particular persons. Those that are called and sanctified are to attribute it alone to the good pleasure of God's goodness, by which they are distinguished. He is sovereign, and hath mercy on whom he will have mercy.

Man hath now a greater dependence on the grace of God than he had before the fall. He depends on the free goodness of God for much more than he did then. Then he depended on God's goodness for conferring the reward of perfect obedience; for God was not obliged to promise and bestow that reward. But now we are dependent on the grace of God for much more; we stand in need of grace, not only to bestow glory upon us, but to deliver us from Hell and eternal wrath. Under the first covenant we depended on God's goodness to give us the reward of righteousness; and so we do now; but we stand in need of God's free and sovereign grace to give us that righteousness; to pardon our sin, and release us from the guilt and infinite demerit of it.

And as we are dependent on the goodness of God for more now than under the first covenant, so we are dependent on a much greater, more free and wonderful goodness. We are now more dependent on God's arbitrary and sovereign good pleasure. We were in our first estate dependent on God for holiness. We had our original righteousness from him; but then holiness was not bestowed in such a way of sovereign good pleasure as it is now. Man was created holy, for it became God to create holy all his reasonable creatures. It would have been a disparagement to the holiness of God's nature, if he had made an intelligent creature unholy. But now when fallen man is made holy, it is from mere and arbitrary grace; God may forever deny holiness to the fallen creature if he pleases, without any disparagement to any of his perfections.

And we are not only indeed more dependent on the grace of God, but our dependence is much more conspicuous, because our own insufficiency and helplessness in ourselves is much more apparent in our fallen and undone state, than it was before we were either sinful or miserable. We are more apparently dependent on God for holiness, because we are first sinful, and utterly polluted, and afterward holy. So the production of the effect is sensible, and its derivation from God more obvious. If man was ever holy and always was so, it would not be so apparent, that he had not holiness necessarily, as an inseparable qualification of human nature. So we are more apparently dependent on free grace for the favor of God, for we are first justly the objects of his displeasure, and afterwards are received into favor. We are more apparently dependent on God for happiness, being first miserable, and afterwards happy. It is more apparently free and without merit in us, because we are actually without any kind of excellency to merit, if there could be any such thing as merit in creature excellency. And we are not only without any true excellency, but are full of, and wholly defiled with, that which is infinitely odious. All our good is more apparently from God, because we are first naked and wholly without any good, and afterwards enriched with all good.

Secondly, we receive all from the power *of God.* Man's redemption is often spoken of as a work of wonderful power as well as grace. The great power of God appears in bringing a sinner from his low state, from the depths of sin and misery, to such an exalted state of holiness and happiness. Eph. 1:19: "And what is the exceeding greatness of his power to us-ward, who believe, according to the working of his mighty power."

We are dependent on God's power through every step of our redemption. We are dependent on the power of God to convert us, and give faith in Jesus Christ, and the new nature.

> It is a work of creation:
>
> "If any man be in Christ, he is a new creature," (2 Cor. 5:17). "We are created in Christ Jesus," (Eph. 2:10).

The fallen creature cannot attain to true holiness, but by being created again. Eph. 4:24:

> "And that ye put on the new man, which after God is created in righteousness and true holiness."

It is a raising from the dead. Colos. 2:12–13:

> "Wherein also ye are risen with him through the faith of the operation of God, who hath raised him from the dead."

Yea, it is a more glorious work of power than mere creation, or raising a dead body to life, in that the effect attained is greater and more excellent. That holy and happy being, and spiritual life, which is produced in the work of conversion, is a far greater and more glorious effect, than mere being and life. And the state from whence the change is made—a death in sin, a total corruption of nature, and depth of misery—is far more remote from the state attained, than mere death or non-entity.

It is by God's power also that we are preserved in a state of grace. 1 Pet. 1:5: "Who are kept by the power of God through faith unto salvation." As grace is at first from God, so it is continually from him, and is maintained by him, as much as light in the atmosphere is all day long from the sun, as well as at first dawning, or sun-rising. Men are dependent on the power of God for every exercise of grace, and for carrying on that work in the heart, for subduing sin and corruption, increasing holy principles, and enabling to bring forth fruit in good works. Man is dependent on divine power in bringing grace to its perfection, in making the soul completely amiable in Christ's glorious likeness, and filling of it with a satisfying joy and blessedness; and for the raising of the body to life, and to such a perfect state, that it shall be suitable for a habitation and organ for a soul so perfected and blessed. These are the most glorious effects of the power of God, that are seen in the series of God's acts with respect to the creatures.

Man was dependent on the power of God in his first estate, but he is more dependent on his power now; he needs God's power to do more things for him, and depends on a more wonderful exercise of his power. It was an effect of the power of God to make man holy at the first: but more remarkably so now, because there is a great deal of opposition and difficulty in the way. It is a more glorious effect of power to make that holy that was so depraved, and under the dominion of sin, than to confer holiness on that which before had nothing of the contrary. It is a more glorious work of power to rescue a soul out of the hands of the devil, and from the powers of darkness, and to bring it into a state of salvation, than to confer holiness where there was no prepossession or opposition. Luke 11:21–22:

> When a strong man armed keepeth his palace, his goods are in peace; but when a stronger than he shall come upon him, and overcome him, he taketh from him all his armor, wherein he trusted, and divideth his spoils.

So it is a more glorious work of power to uphold a soul in a state of grace and holiness, and to carry it on till it is brought to glory, when there is so much sin remaining in the heart resisting, and Satan with all his might opposing, than it would have been to have kept man from falling at first, when Satan had nothing in man.

Thus we have shown how the redeemed are dependent on God for all their good, as they have all of him.

2. *They are also dependent on God for all, as they have all through him.* God is the medium of it, as well as the author and fountain of it. All we have, wisdom, the pardon of sin, deliverance from Hell, acceptance into God's favor, grace and holiness, true comfort and happiness, eternal life and glory, is from God by a Mediator; and this Mediator is God; which Mediator we have an absolute dependence upon, as he through whom we receive all. So that here is another way wherein we have our dependence on God for all good. God not only gives us the Mediator, and accepts his mediation, and of his power and grace bestows the things purchased by the Mediator; but he the Mediator is God.

Our blessings are what we have by purchase; and the purchase is made of God, the blessings are purchased of him, and God gives the purchaser; and not only so, but God is the purchaser. Yea, God is both the purchaser and the price; for Christ, who is God, purchased these blessings for us, by offering up himself as the price of our salvation. He purchased eternal life by the sacrifice of himself. Heb. 7:27: "He offered up himself." And 9:26: "He hath appeared to take away sin by the sacrifice of himself." Indeed it was the human nature that was offered; but it was the same person with the divine, and therefore was an infinite price.

As we thus have our good through God, we have a dependence on him in a respect that man in his first estate had not. Man was to have eternal life then through his own righteousness; so that he had partly a dependence upon what was in himself; for we have a dependence upon that through which we have our good, as well as that from which we have it; and though man's righteousness that he then depended on was indeed from God, yet it was his own, it was inherent in himself; so that his dependence was not so *immediately* on God. But now the righteousness that we are dependent on is not in ourselves, but in God. We are saved through the righteousness of Christ: He *is made unto us righteousness;* and therefore is prophesied of, Jer. 23:6, under that name, "the Lord our righteousness." In that the righteousness we are justified by is the righteousness of Christ: it is the righteousness of God. 2 Cor.5:21: "That we might be made the righteousness of God in him."

Thus, in redemption we have not only all things *of* God, but *by* and *through* him. 1 Cor. 8:6:

> But to us there is but one God, the Father, of whom are all things, and we in him; and one Lord Jesus Christ, by whom are all things, and we by him.

3. *The redeemed have all their good in God.* We not only have it of him, and through him, but it consists in him; he is all our good.

The good of the redeemed is either objective or inherent. By their objective good, I mean that extrinsic object, in the possession and enjoyment of which they are happy. Their inherent good is that excellency or pleasure which is in the soul itself. With respect to both of which the redeemed have all their good in God, or which is the same thing, God himself is all their good.

Firstly, the redeemed have all their objective *good in God.* God himself is the great good which they are brought to the possession and enjoyment of by redemption. He is the highest good, and the sum of all that good which Christ purchased. God is the inheritance of the saints; he is the portion of their souls. God is their wealth and treasure, their food, their Life, their dwelling-place, their ornament and diadem, and their everlasting honor and glory. They have none in heaven but God; he is the great good which the redeemed are received to at death, and which they are to rise to at the end of the world. The Lord God is the light of the heavenly Jerusalem; and is the "river of the water of life" that runs, and "the tree of life that grows, in the midst of the paradise of God." The glorious excellencies and beauty of God will be what will forever entertain the minds of the saints, and the love of God will be their everlasting feast. The redeemed will indeed enjoy other things; they will enjoy the angels, and will enjoy one another; but that which they shall enjoy in the angels, or each other, or in anything else whatsoever that will yield them delight and happiness, will be what shall be seen of God in them.

Secondly, the redeemed have all their inherent *good in God.* Inherent good is twofold; it is either excellency or pleasure. These the redeemed not only derive from God, as caused by him, but have them in him. They have spiritual excellency and joy by a kind of participation of God. They are made excellent by a communication of God's excellency. God puts his own beauty, *i.e.* his beautiful likeness, upon their souls. They are made partakers of the divine nature, or moral image of God, (2 Pet. 1:4). They are holy by being made partakers of God's holiness, (Heb. 12:10.) The saints are beautiful and blessed by a communication of God's holiness and joy, as the moon and planets are bright by the sun's light. The saint hath spiritual joy and pleasure by a kind of effusion of God on the soul. In these things the redeemed have communion with God; that is, they partake with him and of him.

The saints have both their spiritual excellency and blessedness by the gift of the Holy Ghost, and his dwelling in them. They are not only caused by the Holy Ghost, but are in him as their principle. The Holy Spirit becoming an inhabitant is a vital principle in the soul. He, acting in, upon, and with the soul, becomes a fountain of true holiness and joy, as a spring is of water, by the exertion and diffusion of itself. John 4:14:

> But whosoever drinketh of the water that I shall give him, shall never thirst; but the water that I shall give him, shall be in him a well of water springing up into everlasting life.

Compared with chap. 7:38–39:

> He that believeth on me, as the Scripture hath said, out of his belly shall flow rivers of living water; but this spake he of the Spirit, which they that believe on him should receive.

The sum of what Christ has purchased for us is that spring of water spoken of in the former of those places, and those rivers of living water spoken of in the latter. And the sum of the blessings, which the redeemed shall receive in heaven, is that river of water of life that proceeds from the throne of God and the Lamb (Rev. 22:1). Which doubtless signifies the same with those rivers of living water, explained in John 7:38–39, which is elsewhere called the "river of God's pleasures." Herein consists the fullness of good, which the saints receive of Christ. It is by partaking of the Holy Spirit, that they have communion with Christ in his fullness. God hath given the Spirit, not by measure unto him; and they do receive of his fullness, and grace for grace. This is the sum of the saints' inheritance; and therefore that little of the Holy Ghost which believers have in this world, is said to be the earnest of their inheritance. 2 Cor. 1:22: "Who hath also sealed us, and given us the earnest of the Spirit in our hearts." And chap. 5:5: "Now he that hath wrought us for the self-same thing, is God, who also hath given unto us the earnest of the Spirit." And Eph. 1:13–14: "Ye were sealed with that holy Spirit of promise, which is the earnest of our inheritance, until the redemption of the purchased possession."

The Holy Spirit and good things are spoken of in Scripture as the same; as if the Spirit of God communicated to the soul, comprised all good things. Matt. 7:11: "How much more shall your heavenly Father give good things to them that ask him?" In Luke, it is chap. 11:13: "How much more shall your heavenly Father give the Holy Spirit to them that ask him?"

This is the sum of the blessings that Christ died to procure, and the subject of gospel-promises. Gal. 3:13–14: "He was made a curse for us, that we might receive the promise of the Spirit through faith." The Spirit of God is the great promise of the Father. Luke 24:49: "Behold, I send the promise of my Father upon you." The Spirit of God therefore is called "the Spirit of promise" (Eph. 1:33).

This promised thing Christ received, and had given into his hand, as soon as he had finished the work of our redemption, to bestow on all that he had redeemed. Acts 2:13:

> Therefore being by the right hand of God exalted, and having received of the Father the promise of the Holy Ghost, he hath shed forth this, which ye both see and hear.

So that all the holiness and happiness of the redeemed is in God. It is in the communications, indwelling, and acting of the Spirit of God. Holiness and happiness is in the fruit, here and hereafter, because God dwells in them, and they in God.

Thus God has given us the Redeemer, and it is by him that our good is purchased. So God is the Redeemer and the price; and he also is the good purchased. So that all that we have is of God, and through him, and in him. Rom. 11:36: "For of him, and through him, and to him, or in him, are all things." The same in the Greek that is here rendered *to him*, is rendered *in him*, 1 Cor. 8:6.

II. God is glorified in the work of redemption by this means, viz. by there being so great and universal a dependence of the redeemed on him.

1. *Man hath so much the greater occasion and obligation to notice and acknowledge God's perfections and all-sufficiency.* The greater the creature's dependence is on God's perfections, and the greater concern he has with them, so much the greater occasion has he to take notice of them. So much the greater concern anyone has with and dependence upon the power and grace of God, so much the greater occasion has he to take notice of that power and grace. So much the greater and more immediate dependence there is on the divine holiness, so much the greater occasion to take notice of and acknowledge that. So much the greater and more absolute dependence we have on the divine perfections, as belonging to the several persons of the Trinity, so much the greater occasion have we to observe and own the divine glory of each of them. That which we are most concerned with, is surely most in the way of our observation and notice; and this kind of concern with anything, viz. dependence, does especially tend to command and oblige the attention and observation. Those things that we are not much dependent upon, it is easy to neglect; but we can scarce do any other than mind that which we have a great dependence on. By reason of our so great dependence on God, and his

perfections, and in so many respects, he and his glory are the more directly set in our view, which way soever we turn our eyes.

We have the greater occasion to take notice of God's all-sufficiency, when all our sufficiency is thus every way of him. We have the more occasion to contemplate him as an infinite good, and as the fountain of all good. Such a dependence on God demonstrates his all-sufficiency. So much as the dependence of the creature is on God, so much the greater does the creature's emptiness in himself appear; and so much the greater the creature's emptiness, so much the greater must the fullness of the Being be who supplies him. Our having all *of* God, shows the fullness of his power and grace; our having all *through* him, shows the fullness of his merit and worthiness; and our having all *in* him, demonstrates his fullness of beauty, love, and happiness. And the redeemed, by reason of the greatness of their dependence on God, have not only so much the greater occasion, but obligation to contemplate and acknowledge the glory and fullness of God. How unreasonable and ungrateful should we be, if we did not acknowledge that sufficiency and glory which we absolutely, immediately, and universally depend upon!

2. *Hereby is demonstrated how great God's glory is considered comparatively, or as compared with the creature's.* By the creature being thus wholly and universally dependent on God, it appears that the creature is nothing, and that God is all. Hereby it appears that God is infinitely above us; that God's strength, and wisdom, and holiness, are infinitely greater than ours. However great and glorious the creature apprehends God to be, yet if he be not sensible of the difference between God and him, so as to see that God's glory is great, compared with his own, he will not be disposed to give God the glory due to his name. If the creature in any respects sets himself upon a level with God, or exalts himself to any competition with him, however he may apprehend that great honor and profound respect may belong to God from those that are at a greater distance, he will not be so sensible of its being due from him. So much the more men exalt themselves, so much the less will they surely be disposed to exalt God. It is certainly what God aims at in the disposition of things in redemption, (if we allow the Scriptures to be a revelation of God's mind,) that God should appear full, and man in himself empty, that God should appear all, and man nothing. It is God's declared design that others should not "glory in his presence;" which implies that it is his design to advance his own comparative glory. So much the more man "glories in God's presence," so much the less glory is ascribed to God.

3. *By its being thus ordered, that the creature should have so absolute and universal a dependence on God, provision is made that God should have our whole souls, and should be the object of our undivided respect.* If we had our dependence partly on God, and partly on something else, man's respect would be divided to those different things on which he had dependence. Thus it would be if we depended on God only for a part of our good, and on ourselves, or some other being, for another part: or if we had our good only from God, and through another that was not God, and in something else distinct from both, our hearts would be divided between the good itself, and him from whom, and him through whom, we received it. But now there is no occasion for this, God being not only he from or of whom we have all good, but also through whom, and is that good itself, that we have from him and through him. So that whatsoever there is to attract our respect, the tendency is still directly towards God; all unites in him as the center.

Use/Application

1. *We may here observe the marvelous wisdom of God, in the work of redemption.* God hath made man's emptiness and misery, his low, lost, and ruined state, into which he sunk by the fall, an occasion of the greater advancement of his own glory, as in other ways, so particularly in this, that there is now much more universal and apparent dependence of man on God. Though God be pleased to lift man out of that dismal abyss of sin and woe into which he was fallen, and exceedingly to exalt him in excellency and honor, and to a high pitch of glory and blessedness, yet the creature hath nothing in any respect to glory of; all the glory evidently belongs to God, all is in a mere, and most absolute, and divine dependence on the Father, Son, and Holy Ghost. And each person of the Trinity is equally glorified in this work: there is an absolute dependence of the creature on every one for all: all is of the Father, all through the Son, and all in the Holy Ghost. Thus God appears in the work of redemption as all in all. It is fit that he who is, and there is none else, should be the Alpha and Omega, the first and the last, the all and the only, in this work.

2. *Hence those doctrines and schemes of divinity that are in any respect opposite to such an absolute and universal dependence on God, derogate from his glory, and thwart the design of our redemption.* And such are those schemes that put the creature in God's stead, in any of the mentioned respects, that exalt man into the place of either Father, Son, or Holy Ghost, in anything

pertaining to our redemption. However they may allow of a dependence of the redeemed on God, yet they deny a dependence that is so absolute and universal. They own an entire dependence of God for some things, but not for others; they own that we depend on God for the gift and acceptance of a Redeemer, but deny so absolute a dependence on him for the obtaining of an *interest* in the Redeemer. They own an absolute dependence on the Father for giving his Son, and on the Son for working out redemption, but not so entire a dependence on the Holy Ghost for *conversion*, and a being in Christ, and so coming to a title to his benefits. They own a dependence on God for means of grace, but not absolutely for the benefit and success of those means; a partial dependence on the power of God, for obtaining and exercising holiness, but not a mere dependence on the arbitrary and sovereign grace of God. They own a dependence on the free grace of God for a reception into his favor, so far that it is without any proper merit, but not as it is without being attracted, or moved with any excellency. They own a partial dependence on Christ, as he through whom we have life, as having purchased new terms of life, but still hold that the righteousness through which we have life is inherent in ourselves, as it was under the first covenant. Now whatever scheme is inconsistent with our *entire* dependence on God for all, and of having all of him, through him, and in him, it is repugnant to the design and tenor of the gospel, and robs it of that which God accounts its luster and glory.

3. *Hence we may learn a reason why faith is that by which we come to have an interest in this redemption; for there is included in the nature of faith, a sensible acknowledgment of absolute dependence on God in this affair.* It is very fit that it should be required of all, in order to their having the benefit of this redemption, that they should be sensible of, and acknowledge, their dependence on God for it. It is by this means that God hath contrived to glorify himself in redemption; and it is fit that he should at least have this glory of those that are the subjects of this redemption, and have the benefit of it.

Faith is a sensibleness of what is real in the work of redemption; and the soul that believes doth entirely depend on God for all salvation, in its own sense and act. Faith abases men, and exalts God; it gives all the glory of redemption to him alone. It is necessary in order to saving faith, that man should be emptied of himself, be sensible that he is "wretched, and miserable, and poor, and blind, and naked." Humility is a great ingredient of true faith: he that truly receives redemption, receives it as a little child, Mark 10:15. "Whosoever shall not receive the kingdom of heaven as a little child, he shall not enter therein." It is the delight of a believing soul to abase itself and exalt God alone: that is the language of it, Psalm 115:1. "Not unto us, O Lord, not unto us, but to thy name give glory."

4. *Let us be exhorted to exalt God alone, and ascribe to him all the glory of redemption.* Let us endeavor to obtain, and increase in, a sensibleness of our great dependence on God, to have our eye to him alone, to mortify a self-dependent and self-righteous disposition. Man is naturally exceeding prone to exalt himself, and depend on his own power or goodness; as though from himself he must expect happiness. He is prone to have respect to enjoyments alien from God and his Spirit, as those in which happiness is to be found.

But this doctrine should teach us to exalt God *alone*; as by trust and reliance, so by praise. *Let him that glorieth, glory in the Lord.* Hath any man hope that he is converted, and sanctified, and that his mind is endowed with true excellency and spiritual beauty? That his sins are forgiven, and he received into God's favor, and exalted to the honor and blessedness of being his child, and an heir of eternal life? Let him give God all the glory; who alone makes him to differ from the worst of men in this world, or the most miserable of the damned in Hell. Hath any man much comfort and strong hope of eternal life, let not his hope lift him up, but dispose him the more to abase himself, to reflect on his own exceeding unworthiness of such a favor, and to exalt God alone. Is any man eminent in holiness, and abundant in good works, let him take nothing of the glory of it to himself, but ascribe it to him whose "workmanship we are, created in Christ Jesus unto good works."

God's Sovereignty in the Salvation of Men

Originally preached circa August 1731–December 1732.

"Therefore hath he mercy on whom he will have mercy, and whom he will, he hardeneth."—Romans 9:18

The apostle, in the beginning of this chapter, expresses his great concern and sorrow of heart for the nation of the Jews, who were rejected of God. This leads him to observe the difference which God made by election between some of the Jews and others, and between the bulk of that people and the Christian Gentiles. In speaking of this he enters into a more minute discussion of the sovereignty of God in electing some to eternal life, and rejecting others, than is found in any other part of the Bible; in the course of which he quotes several passages from the Old Testament, confirming and illustrating this doctrine.

In the ninth verse he refers us to what God said to Abraham, showing his election of Isaac before Ishmael: "For this is the word of promise; At this time will I come, and Sarah shall have a son;" then to what God had said to Rebecca, showing his election of Jacob before Esau; "The elder shall serve the younger." In the thirteenth verse, [he refers] to a passage from Malachi, "Jacob have I loved, but Esau have I hated."

In the fifteenth verse, to what God said to Moses, "I will have mercy on whom I will have mercy; and I will have compassion on whom I will have compassion."

In the verse preceding the text, [he refers] to what God says to Pharaoh:

> "For the scripture saith unto Pharaoh, 'Even for this same purpose have I raised thee up, that I might show my power in thee, and that my name might be declared throughout all the earth.' "

In what the apostle says in the text, he seems to have respect [referred] especially to the two last-cited passages: to what God said to Moses in the fifteenth verse, and to what he said to Pharaoh in the verse immediately preceding. God said to Moses, "I will have mercy on whom I will have mercy." To this the apostle refers in the former part of the text. And we know how often it is said of Pharaoh, that God hardened his heart. And to this the apostle seems to have respect in the latter part of the text; "and whom he will he hardeneth." We may observe in the text,

1. *God's different dealing with men.* He hath mercy on some, and hardeneth others. When God is here spoken of as hardening some of the children of men, it is not to be understood that God by any positive efficiency hardens any man's heart. There is no positive act in God [here], as though he put forth any power to harden the heart. To suppose any such thing would be to make God the immediate author of sin. God is said to harden men in two ways: by withholding the powerful influences of his Spirit, without which their hearts will remain hardened, and grow harder and harder: in this sense he hardens them, as he leaves them to hardness. And again, by ordering those things in his providence which, through the abuse of their corruption, become the occasion of their hardening. Thus God sends his word and ordinances to men which, by their abuse, prove an occasion of their hardening. So the apostle said, that he was unto some "a savior of death unto death." So God is represented as sending Isaiah on this errand, to make the hearts of the people fat, and to make their ears heavy, and to shut their eyes; lest they should see with their eyes, and hear with their ears, and understand with their heart, and convert, and be healed. (Isa. 6:10.) Isaiah's preaching was, in itself, of a contrary tendency, to make them better. But their abuse of it rendered it an occasion of their hardening. As God is here said to harden men, so he is said to put a lying spirit in the mouth of the false prophets. (2 Chron. 18:22.) That is, he suffered a lying

spirit to enter into them. And thus he is said to have bid Shimei curse David. (2 Sam. 16:10.) Not that he properly commanded him; for it is contrary to God's commands. God expressly forbids cursing the ruler of the people. (Exod. 22:28.) But he suffered corruption at that time so to work in Shimei, and ordered that occasion of stirring it up, as a manifestation of his displeasure against David.

2. *The foundation of his different dealing with mankind; viz. his sovereign will and pleasure.* "He hath mercy on whom he will have mercy, and whom he will, he hardeneth." This does not imply, merely, that God never shows mercy or denies it against his will, or that he is always willing to do it when he does it. A willing subject or servant, when he obeys his lord's commands, may never do anything against his will, nothing but what he can do cheerfully and with delight; and yet he cannot be said to do what he wills in the sense of the text. But the expression implies that it is God's mere will and sovereign pleasure, which supremely orders this affair. It is the divine will without restraint, or constraint, or obligation.

***Doctrine.* God exercises his sovereignty in the eternal salvation of men.**

He not only is sovereign, and has a sovereign right to dispose and order in that affair; and he not only might proceed in a sovereign way, if he would, and nobody could charge him with exceeding his right; but he actually *does so*; he exercises the right which he has. In the following discourse, I propose to show,

I. I would show what is God's sovereignty.

The sovereignty of God is his absolute, independent right of disposing of all creatures according to his own pleasure. I will consider this definition by the parts of it.

The will of God is called his *mere pleasure,*

1. *In opposition to any constraint.* Men may do things voluntarily, and yet there may be a degree of constraint. A man may be said to do a thing voluntarily, that is, he himself does it; and, all things considered, he may choose to do it; yet he may do it out of fear, and the thing in itself considered be irksome to him, and sorely against his inclination. When men do things thus, they cannot be said to do them according to their mere pleasure.

2. *In opposition to its being under the will of another.* A servant may fulfill his master's commands, and may do it willingly, and cheerfully, and may

delight to do his master's will; yet when he does so, he does not do it of his own mere pleasure. The saints do the will of God freely. They choose to do it; it is their meat and drink. Yet they do not do it of their mere pleasure and arbitrary will; because their will is under the direction of a superior will.

3. *In opposition to any proper obligation.* A man may do a thing which he is obliged to do, very freely; but he cannot be said to act from his own mere will and pleasure. He who acts from his own mere pleasure, is at full liberty; but he who is under any proper obligation, is not at liberty, but is bound.

Now the sovereignty of God supposes, that he has a right to dispose of all his creatures according to his mere pleasure in the sense explained. And his right is absolute and independent. Men may have a right to dispose of some things according to their pleasure. But their right is not absolute and unlimited. Men may be said to have a right to dispose of their own goods as they please. But their right is not absolute; it has limits and bounds. They have a right to dispose of their own goods as they please, provided they do not do it contrary to the law of the state to which they are subject, or contrary to the law of God. Men's right to dispose of their things as they will, is not absolute, because it is not independent. They have not an independent right to what they have, but in some things depend on the community to which they belong, for the right they have; and in everything depend on God. They receive all the right they have to anything from God. But the sovereignty of God imports that he has an absolute, and unlimited, and independent right of disposing of his creatures as he will.

II. I proposed to inquire, what God's sovereignty in the salvation of men implies.

In answer to this inquiry, I observe, it implies that God can either bestow salvation on any of the children of men, or refuse it, without any prejudice to the glory of any of his attributes, except where he has been pleased to declare, that he will or will not bestow it. It cannot be said absolutely, as the case now stands, that God can, without any prejudice to the honor of any of his attributes, bestow salvation on any of the children of men, or refuse it; because, concerning some, God has been pleased to declare either that he will, or that he will not bestow salvation on them; and thus to bind himself by his own promise. And concerning some, he has been pleased to declare that he never will bestow salvation upon them; viz. those who have committed the sin against the Holy Ghost. Hence, as the case now stands, he is obliged; he cannot bestow salvation in one case, or refuse it in the other, without prejudice to the honor of his truth. But God exercised his sovereignty in making these declarations. God was not obliged to promise that he would save all who believe in Christ; nor was he obliged to declare, that he who committed the sin against the Holy Ghost should never be forgiven. But it pleased him so to declare. And had it not been so that God had been pleased to oblige himself in these cases, he might still have either bestowed salvation, or refused it, without prejudice to any of his attributes. If it would in itself be prejudicial to any of his attributes to bestow or refuse salvation, then God would not in that matter act as absolutely sovereign. Because it then ceases to be a merely arbitrary thing. It ceases to be a matter of absolute liberty, and is become a matter of necessity or obligation. For God cannot do anything to the prejudice of any of his attributes, or contrary to what is in itself excellent and glorious. Therefore,

1. *God can, without prejudice to the glory of any of his attributes, bestow salvation on any of the children of men, except on those who have committed the sin against the Holy Ghost.* The case was thus when man fell, and before God revealed his eternal purpose and plan for redeeming men by Jesus Christ. It was probably looked upon by the angels as a thing utterly inconsistent with God's attributes to save any of the children of men. It was utterly inconsistent with the honor of the divine attributes to save any one of the fallen children of men, as they were in themselves. It could not have been done had not God contrived a way consistent with the honor of his holiness, majesty, justice, and truth. But since God in the gospel has revealed that nothing is too hard for him to do, nothing beyond the reach of his power, and wisdom, and sufficiency; and since Christ has wrought out the work of redemption, and fulfilled the law by obeying, there is none of mankind whom he may not save without any prejudice to any of his attributes, excepting those who have committed the sin against the Holy Ghost. And those he might have saved without going contrary to any of his attributes, had he not been pleased to declare that he would not. It was not because he could not have saved them consistently with his justice, and consistently with his law, or because his attribute of mercy was not great enough, or the blood of Christ not sufficient to cleanse from that sin. But it has pleased him for wise reasons to declare that that sin shall never be forgiven in this world, or in the world to come. And so now it is contrary to God's truth to save such. But otherwise there is no sinner, let him be ever so great, but God can save him without prejudice to any attribute; if he has been a murderer, adulterer, or perjurer, or idolater, or blasphemer, God may save him if he

pleases, and in no respect injure his glory. Though persons have sinned long, have been obstinate, have committed heinous sins a thousand times, even till they have grown old in sin, and have sinned under great aggravations: let the aggravations be what they may; if they have sinned under ever so great light; if they have been backsliders, and have sinned against ever so numerous and solemn warnings and strivings of the Spirit, and mercies of his common providence: though the danger of such is much greater than of other sinners, yet God can save them if he pleases, for the sake of Christ, without any prejudice to any of his attributes. He may have mercy on whom he will have mercy. He may have mercy on the greatest of sinners, if he pleases, and the glory of none of his attributes will be in the least sullied. Such is the sufficiency of the satisfaction and righteousness of Christ, that none of the divine attributes stand in the way of the salvation of any of them. Thus the glory of any attribute did not at all suffer by Christ's saving some of his crucifiers.

2. *God may save any of them without prejudice to the honor of his holiness.* God is an infinitely holy being. The heavens are not pure in his sight. He is of purer eyes than to behold evil, and cannot look on iniquity. And if God should in any way countenance sin, and should not give proper testimonies of his hatred of it, and displeasure at it, it would be a prejudice to the honor of his holiness. But God can save the greatest sinner without giving the least countenance to sin. If he saves one, who for a long time has stood out under the calls of the gospel, and has sinned under dreadful aggravations; if he saves one who, against light, has been a pirate or blasphemer, he may do it without giving any countenance to their wickedness; because his abhorrence of it and displeasure against it have been already sufficiently manifested in the sufferings of Christ. It was a sufficient testimony of God's abhorrence against even the greatest wickedness, that Christ, the eternal Son of God, died for it. Nothing can show God's infinite abhorrence of any wickedness more than this. If the wicked man himself should be thrust into Hell, and should endure the most extreme torments which are ever suffered there, it would not be a greater manifestation of God's abhorrence of it, than the sufferings of the Son of God for it.

3. *God may save any of the children of men without prejudice to the honor of his majesty.* If men have affronted God, and that ever so much, if they have cast ever so much contempt on his authority; yet God can save them, if he pleases, and the honor of his majesty not suffer in the least. If God should save those who have affronted him, without satisfaction, the honor of his

majesty would suffer. For when contempt is cast upon infinite majesty, its honor suffers, and the contempt leaves an obscurity upon the honor of the divine majesty, if the injury is not repaired. But the sufferings of Christ do fully repair the injury. Let the contempt be ever so great, yet if so honorable a person as Christ undertakes to be a Mediator for the offender, and in the mediation suffer in his stead, it fully repairs the injury done to the majesty of heaven by the greatest sinner.

4. *God may save any sinner whatsoever consistently with his justice.* The justice of God requires the punishment of sin. God is the Supreme Judge of the world, and he is to judge the world according to the rules of justice. It is not the part of a judge to show favor to the person judged; but he is to determine according to a rule of justice without departing to the right hand or left. God does not show mercy as a judge, but as a sovereign. And therefore when mercy sought the salvation of sinners, the inquiry was how to make the exercise of the mercy of God as a sovereign, and of his strict justice as a judge, agree together. And this is done by the sufferings of Christ, in which sin is punished fully, and justice answered. Christ suffered enough for the punishment of the sins of the greatest sinner that ever lived. So that God, when he judges, may act according to a rule of strict justice, and yet acquit the sinner, if he be in Christ. Justice cannot require any more for any man's sins, than those sufferings of one of the persons in the Trinity, which Christ suffered. Rom. 3:25,26:

> Whom God hath set forth to be a propitiation through faith in his blood; to declare his righteousness, that he might be just, and the justifier of him which believeth in Christ."

5. *God can save any sinner whatsoever, without any prejudice to the honor of his truth.* God passed his word, that sin should be punished with death, which is to be understood not only of the first, but of the second death. God can save the greatest sinner consistently with his truth in this threatening. For sin is punished in the sufferings of Christ, inasmuch as he is our surety, and so is legally the same person, and sustained our guilt, and in his sufferings bore our punishment. It may be objected, that God said, "If thou eatest, thou shalt die;" as though the same person that sinned must suffer; and therefore why does not God's truth oblige him to that? I answer, that the word then was not intended to be restrained to him, that in his own person sinned. Adam probably understood that his posterity were included, whether they sinned in their own person or not. If they sinned in Adam, their surety, those words, "if thou eatest," meant, "if thou eatest in thyself,

or in thy surety." And therefore, the latter words, "thou shalt die," do also fairly allow of such a construction as, "thou shalt die in thyself, or in thy surety." Isa. 42:21: "The Lord is well pleased for his righteousness' sake, he will magnify the law and make it honorable."

II. But, God may refuse salvation to any sinner whatsoever, without prejudice to the honor of any of his attributes.

There is no person whatever in a natural condition, upon whom God may not refuse to bestow salvation without prejudice to any part of his glory. Let a natural person be wise or unwise, of a good or ill natural temper, of mean or honorable parentage, whether born of wicked or godly parents; let him be a moral or immoral person, whatever good he may have done, however religious he has been, how many prayers soever he has made, and whatever pains he has taken that he may be saved; whatever concern and distress he may have for fear he shall be damned; or whatever circumstances he may be in; God can deny him salvation without the least disparagement to any of his perfections. His glory will not in any instance be the least obscured by it.

1. *God may deny salvation to any natural person without any injury to the honor of his righteousness.* If he does so, there is no injustice nor unfairness in it. There is no natural man living, let his case be what it will, but God may deny him salvation, and cast him down to Hell, and yet not be chargeable with the least unrighteous or unfair dealing in any respect whatsoever. This is evident, because they all have deserved Hell: and it is no injustice for a proper judge to inflict on any man what he deserves. And as he has deserved condemnation, so he has never done anything to remove the liability, or to atone for the sin. He never has done anything whereby he has laid any obligations on God not to punish him as he deserved.

2. *God may deny salvation to any unconverted person whatever without any prejudice to the honor of his goodness.* Sinners are sometimes ready to flatter themselves, that though it may not be contrary to the justice of God to condemn them, yet it will not consist with the glory of his mercy. They think it will be dishonorable to God's mercy to cast them into Hell, and have no pity or compassion upon them. They think it will be very hard and severe, and not becoming a God of infinite grace and tender compassion. But God can deny salvation to any natural person without any disparagement to his mercy and goodness. That, which is not contrary to God's justice, is not contrary to his mercy. If damnation be justice, then mercy may choose its

own object. They mistake the nature of the mercy of God, who think that it is an attribute, which, in some cases, is contrary to justice. Nay, God's mercy is illustrated by it, as in the twenty-third verse of the context. "That he might make known the riches of his glory on the vessels of mercy, which he had afore prepared unto glory."

3. *It is in no way prejudicial to the honor of God's faithfulness.* For God has in no way obliged himself to any natural man by his word to bestow salvation upon him. Men in a natural condition are not the children of promise; but lie open to the curse of the law, which would not be the case if they had any promise to lay hold of.

III. God does actually exercise his sovereignty in men's salvation.

We shall show how he exercises this right in several particulars.

1. *In calling one people or nation, and giving them the means of grace, and leaving others without them.* According to the divine appointment, salvation is bestowed in connection with the means of grace. God may sometimes make use of very unlikely means, and bestow salvation on men who are under very great disadvantages; but he does not bestow grace wholly without any means. But God exercises his sovereignty in bestowing those means. All mankind are by nature in like circumstances towards God. Yet God greatly distinguishes some from others by the means and advantages which he bestows upon them. The savages, who live in the remote parts of this continent, and are under the grossest heathenish darkness, as well as the inhabitants of Africa, are naturally in exactly similar circumstances towards God with us in this land. They are no more alienated or estranged from God in their natures than we; and God has no more to charge them with. And yet what a vast difference has God made between us and them! In this he has exercised his sovereignty. He did this of old, when he chose but one people, to make them his covenant people, and to give them the means of grace, and left all others, and gave them over to heathenish darkness and the tyranny of the devil, to perish from generation to generation for many hundreds of years. The earth in that time was peopled with many great and mighty nations. There were the Egyptians, a people famed for their wisdom. There were also the Assyrians and Chaldeans, who were great, and wise, and powerful nations. There were the Persians, who by their strength and policy subdued a great part of the world. There were the renowned nations of the Greeks and Romans, who were famed over the whole world for their excellent civil governments, for their wisdom and skill in the arts of peace and war, and who by their military prowess in their turns

subdued and reigned over the world. Those were rejected. God did not choose them for his people, but left them for many ages under gross heathenish darkness, to perish for lack of vision; and chose one only people, the posterity of Jacob, to be his own people, and to give them the means of grace. Psal. 147:19,20:

> He showeth his word unto Jacob, his statutes and his judgments unto Israel. He hath not dealt so with any nation; and as for his judgments, they have not known them.

This nation was a small, inconsiderable people in comparison with many other people. Deut. 7:7: "The Lord did not set his love upon you, nor choose you, because ye were more in number than any people; for ye were the fewest of all people." So neither was it for their righteousness; for they had no more of that than other people. Deut. 9:6: "Understand therefore, that the Lord thy God giveth thee not this good land to possess it for thy righteousness; for thou art a stiff-necked people." God gives them to understand, that it was from no other cause but his free electing love, that he chose them to be his people. That reason is given why God loved them; it was because he loved them. (Deut. 7:8.) Which is as much as to say, it was agreeable to his sovereign pleasure, to set his love upon you.

God also showed his sovereignty in choosing that people, when other nations were rejected, who came of the same progenitors. Thus the children of Isaac were chosen, when the posterity of Ishmael and other sons of Abraham were rejected. So the children of Jacob were chosen, when the posterity of Esau were rejected: as the apostle observes in the seventh verse, "Neither because they are the seed of Abraham, are they all children; but in Isaac shall thy seed be called," and again in verses 10–13:

> And not only this; but when Rebekah also had conceived by one, even by our father Isaac; the children moreover being not yet born, neither having done any good or evil, that the promise of God according to election might stand, not of works, but of him that calleth; it was said unto her, "The elder shall serve the younger." As it is written, "Jacob have I loved, but Esau have I hated."

The apostle has not respect merely to the election of the persons of Isaac and Jacob before Ishmael and Esau; but of their posterity. In the passage already quoted from Malachi, God has respect to the nations, which were the posterity of Esau and Jacob; Mal. 1:2,3:

> "I have loved you," saith the Lord. Yet ye say, "Wherein hast thou loved us?" "Was not Esau Jacob's brother?" saith the Lord: "yet I loved Jacob; and I

hated Esau, and laid his mountains and his heritage waste for the dragons of the wilderness."

God showed his sovereignty, when Christ came, in rejecting the Jews, and calling the Gentiles. God rejected that nation who were the children of Abraham according to the flesh, and had been his peculiar people for so many ages, and who alone possessed the one true God, and chose idolatrous heathen before them, and called them to be his people. When the Messiah came, who was born of their nation, and whom they so much expected, he rejected them. He came to his own, and his own received him not. (John 1:11.) When the glorious dispensation of the gospel came, God passed by the Jews, and called those who had been heathens, to enjoy the privileges of it. They were broken off, that the Gentiles might be grafted on. (Rom. 11:17.) "She is now called beloved, that was not beloved. And more are the children of the desolate, than the children of the married wife. (Isa. 54:1.) The natural children of Abraham are rejected, and God raises up children to Abraham of stones. That nation, which was so honored of God, have now been for many ages rejected, and remain dispersed all over the world, a remarkable monument of divine vengeance. And now God greatly distinguishes some Gentile nations from others, and all according to his sovereign pleasure.

2. *God exercises his sovereignty in the advantages he bestows upon particular persons.* All need salvation alike, and all are, naturally, alike undeserving of it; but he gives some vastly greater advantages for salvation than others. To some he assigns their place in pious and religious families, where they may be well instructed and educated, and have religious parents to dedicate them to God, and put up many prayers for them. God places some under a more powerful ministry than others, and in places where there are more of the outpourings of the Spirit of God. To some he gives much more of the strivings and the awakening influences of the Spirit, than to others. It is according to his mere sovereign pleasure.

3. *God exercises his sovereignty in sometimes bestowing salvation upon the low and mean, and denying it to the wise and great.* Christ in his sovereignty passes by the gates of princes and nobles, and enters some cottage and dwells there, and has communion with its obscure inhabitants. God in his sovereignty withheld salvation from the rich man, who fared sumptuously every day, and bestowed it on poor Lazarus, who sat begging at his gate. God in this way pours contempt on princes, and on all their glittering splendor. So God sometimes passes by wise men, men of great

understanding, learned and great scholars, and bestows salvation on others of weak understanding, who only comprehend some of the plainer parts of Scripture, and the fundamental principles of the Christian religion. Yea, there seem to be fewer great men called, than others. And God in ordering it thus manifests his sovereignty. 1 Cor. 1:26–28:

> For ye see your calling, brethren, how that not many wise men after the flesh, not many mighty, not many noble, are called. But God hath chosen the foolish things of the world to confound the wise; and God hath chosen the weak things of the world to confound the things which are mighty; and base things of the world, and things which are despised, hath God chosen, yea, and things which are not, to bring to naught things that are.

4. *In bestowing salvation on some who have had few advantages.* God sometimes will bless weak means for producing astonishing effects, when more excellent means are not succeeded. God sometimes will withhold salvation from those who are the children of very pious parents, and bestow it on others, who have been brought up in wicked families. Thus we read of a good Abijah in the family of Jeroboam, and of a godly Hezekiah, the son of wicked Ahaz, and of a godly Josiah, the son of a wicked Amon. But on the contrary, of a wicked Amnon and Absalom, the sons of holy David, and that vile Manasseh, the son a good Hezekiah. Sometimes some, who have had eminent means of grace, are rejected, and left to perish, and others, under far less advantages, are saved. Thus the scribes and Pharisees, who had so much light and knowledge of the Scriptures, were mostly rejected, and the poor ignorant publicans saved.

The greater part of those, among whom Christ was much conversant, and who heard him preach, and saw him work miracles from day to day, were left; and the woman of Samaria was taken, and many other Samaritans at the same time, who only heard Christ preach, as he occasionally passed through their city. So the woman of Canaan was taken, who was not of the country of the Jews, and but once saw Jesus Christ. So the Jews, who had seen and heard Christ, and saw his miracles, and with whom the apostles labored so much, were not saved. But the Gentiles, many of them, who, as it were, but transiently heard the glad tidings of salvation, embraced them, and were converted.

5. *God exercises his sovereignty in calling some to salvation, who have been very heinously wicked, and leaving others, who have been moral and religious persons.* The Pharisees were a very strict sect among the Jews. Their religion was extraordinary. (Luke 18:11.) They were not as other men,

extortioners, unjust, or adulterers. There was their morality. They fasted twice a week, and gave tithes of all that they possessed. There was their religion. But yet they were mostly rejected, and the publicans, and harlots, and openly vicious sort of people, entered into the kingdom of God before them. (Matt. 21:31.) The apostle describes his righteousness while a Pharisee in Philip. 3:6: "Touching the righteousness which is of the law, blameless." The rich young man, who came kneeling to Christ, saying, "Good Master, what shall I do, that I may have eternal life," was a moral person. When Christ bade him keep the commandments, he said, and in his own view with sincerity, "All these have I kept from my youth up." He had obviously been brought up in a good family, and was a youth of such amiable manners and correct deportment, that it is said, "Jesus beholding him, loved him." Still he was left; while the thief, that was crucified with Christ, was chosen and called, even on the cross. God sometimes shows his sovereignty by showing mercy to the chief of sinners, on those who have been murderers, and profaners, and blasphemers. And even when they are old, some are called at the eleventh hour. God sometimes shows the sovereignty of his grace by showing mercy to some, who have spent most of their lives in the service of Satan, and have little left to spend in the service of God.

6. *In saving some of those who seek salvation, and not others.* Some who seek salvation, as we know both from Scripture and observation, are soon converted; while others seek a long time, and do not obtain at last. God helps some over the mountains and difficulties which are in the way; he subdues Satan, and delivers them from his temptations: but others are ruined by the temptations with which they meet. Some are never thoroughly awakened; while to others God is pleased to give thorough convictions. Some are left to backsliding hearts; others God causes to hold out to the end. Some are brought off from a confidence in their own righteousness; others never get over that obstruction in their way, as long as they live. And some are converted and saved, who never had so great strivings as some who, notwithstanding, perish.

IV. I come now to give the reasons why God does thus exercise his sovereignty in the eternal salvation of the children of men.

1. *It is agreeable to God's design in the creation of the universe to exercise every attribute, and thus to manifest the glory of each of them.* God's design in the creation was to glorify himself, or to make a discovery of the essential glory of

his nature. It was fit that infinite glory should shine forth; and it was God's original design to make a manifestation of his glory, as it is. Not that it was his design to manifest all his glory to the apprehension of creatures; for it is impossible that the minds of creatures should comprehend it. But it was his design to make a true manifestation of his glory, such as should represent every attribute. If God glorified one attribute, and not another, such manifestation of his glory would be defective; and the representation would not be complete. If all God's attributes are not manifested, the glory of none of them is manifested as it is: for the divine attributes reflect glory on one another. Thus if God's wisdom be manifested, and not his holiness, the glory of his wisdom would not be manifested as it is; for one part of the glory of the attribute of divine wisdom is, that it is a holy wisdom. So if his holiness were manifested, and not his wisdom, the glory of his holiness would not be manifested as it is; for one thing which belongs to the glory of God's holiness is, that it is a wise holiness. So it is with respect to the attributes of mercy and justice. The glory of God's mercy does not appear as it is, unless it is manifested as a just mercy, or as a mercy consistent with justice. And so with respect to God's sovereignty, it reflects glory on all his other attributes. It is part of the glory of God's mercy, that it is sovereign mercy. So all the attributes of God reflect glory on one another. The glory of one attribute cannot be manifested, as it is, without the manifestation of another. One attribute is defective without another, and therefore the manifestation will be defective. Hence it was the will of God to manifest all his attributes. The declarative glory of God in Scripture is often called God's *name*, because it declares his nature. But if his name does not signify his nature as it is, or does not declare any attribute, it is not a true name. The sovereignty of God is one of his attributes, and a part of his glory. The glory of God eminently appears in his absolute sovereignty over all creatures, great and small. If the glory of a prince be his power and dominion, then the glory of God is his absolute sovereignty. Herein appear God's infinite greatness and highness above all creatures. Therefore it is the will of God to manifest his sovereignty. And his sovereignty, like his other attributes, is manifested in the exercises of it. He glorifies his power in the exercise of power. He glorifies his mercy in the exercise of mercy. So he glorifies his sovereignty in the exercise of sovereignty.

2. *The more excellent the creature is over whom God is sovereign, and the greater the matter in which he so appears, the more glorious is his sovereignty.* The sovereignty of God in his being sovereign over men, is more glorious than

in his being sovereign over the inferior creatures. And his sovereignty over angels is yet more glorious that his sovereignty over men. For the nobler the creature is, still the greater and higher doth God appear in his sovereignty over it. It is a greater honor to a man to have dominion over men, that over beasts; and a still greater honor to have dominion over princes, nobles, and kings, than over ordinary men. So the glory of God's sovereignty appears in that he is sovereign over the souls of men, who are so noble and excellent creatures. God therefore will exercise his sovereignty over them. And the further the dominion of anyone extends over another, the greater will be the honor. If a man has dominion over another only in some instances, he is not therein so much exalted, as in having absolute dominion over his life, and fortune, and all he has. So God's sovereignty over men appears glorious, that it extends to everything which concerns them. He may dispose of them with respect to all that concerns them, according to his own pleasure. His sovereignty appears glorious, that it reaches their most important affairs, even the eternal state and condition of the souls of men. Herein it appears that the sovereignty of God is without bounds or limits, in that it reaches to an affair of such infinite importance. God, therefore, as it is his design to manifest his own glory, will and does exercise his sovereignty towards men, over their souls and bodies, even in this most important matter of their eternal salvation. He has mercy on whom he will have mercy, and whom he will, he hardens.

Application

1. *Hence we learn how absolutely we are dependent on God in this great matter of the eternal salvation of our souls.* We are dependent not only on his wisdom to contrive a way to accomplish it, and on his power to bring it to pass, but we are dependent on his mere will and pleasure in the affair. We depend on the sovereign will of God for every thing belonging to it, from the foundation to the top-stone. It was of the sovereign pleasure of God, that he contrived a way to save any of mankind, and gave us Jesus Christ, his only-begotten Son, to be our Redeemer. Why did he look on us, and send us a Savior, and not the fallen angels? It was from the sovereign pleasure of God. It was of his sovereign pleasure what means to appoint. His giving us the Bible, and the ordinances of religion, is of his sovereign grace. His giving those means to us rather than to others, his giving the awakening influences of his Spirit, and his bestowing saving grace, are all of his sovereign

pleasure. When he says, "Let there be light in the soul of such an one," it is a word of infinite power and sovereign grace.

2. *Let us with the greatest humility adore the awful and absolute sovereignty of God.* As we have just shown, it is an eminent attribute of the Divine Being, that he is sovereign over such excellent beings as the souls of men, and that in every respect, even in that of their eternal salvation. The infinite greatness of God, and his exaltation above us, appears in nothing more than in his sovereignty. It is spoken of in Scripture as a great part of his glory.

> See now that I, even I, am he, and there is no God with me. I kill, and I make alive; I wound, and I heal; neither is there any that can deliver out of my hand. (Deut. 32:39)

> Our God is in the heavens; he hath done whatsoever he pleased. (Psal. 115:3)

> Whose dominion is an everlasting dominion, and his kingdom is from generation to generation. And all the inhabitants of the earth are reputed as nothing; and he doeth according to his will in the armies of heaven, and among the inhabitants of the earth; and none can stay his hand, or say unto him, "What doest thou?" (Daniel 4:34,35)

Our Lord Jesus Christ praised and glorified the Father for the exercise of his sovereignty in the salvation of men.

> I thank thee, O Father, Lord of heaven and earth, because thou hast hid these things from the wise and prudent, and hast revealed them unto babes. Even so, Father, for so it seemed good in thy sight. (Matt. 11:25,26)

Let us therefore give God the glory of his sovereignty, as adoring him, whose sovereign will orders all things, beholding ourselves as nothing in comparison with him. Dominion and sovereignty require humble reverence and honor in the subject. The absolute, universal, and unlimited sovereignty of God requires, that we should adore him with all possible humility and reverence. It is impossible that we should go to excess in lowliness and reverence of that Being, who may dispose of us to all eternity, as he pleases.

3. *Those who are in a state of salvation are to attribute it to sovereign grace alone, and to give all the praise to him, who maketh them to differ from others.* Godliness is no cause for glorying, except it be in God. 1 Cor. 1:29,30,31:

> That no flesh should glory in his presence. But of him are ye in Christ Jesus, who of God is made unto us wisdom, and righteousness, and sanctification, and redemption. That, according as it is written, "He that glorieth, let him glory in the Lord."

Such are not, by any means, in any degree to attribute their godliness, their safe and happy state and condition, to any natural difference between them and other men, or to any strength or righteousness of their own. They have no reason to exalt themselves in the least degree; but God is the being whom they should exalt. They should exalt God the Father, who chose them in Christ, who set his love upon them, and gave them salvation, before they were born, and even before the world was. If they inquire, why God set his love on them, and chose them rather than others, if they think they can see any cause out of God, they are greatly mistaken. They should exalt God the Son, who bore their names on his heart, when he came into the world, and hung on the cross, and in whom alone they have righteousness and strength. They should exalt God the Holy Ghost, who of sovereign grace has called them out of darkness into marvelous light; who has by his own immediate and free operation, led them into an understanding of the evil and danger of sin, and brought them off from their own righteousness, and opened their eyes to discover the glory of God, and the wonderful riches of God in Jesus Christ, and has sanctified them, and made them new creatures. When they hear of the wickedness of others, or look upon vicious persons, they should think how wicked they once were, and how much they provoked God, and how they deserved forever to be left by him to perish in sin, and that it is only sovereign grace which has made the difference. 1 Cor. 6:10. Many sorts of sinners are there enumerated; fornicators, idolaters, adulterers, effeminate, abusers of themselves with mankind. And then in the eleventh verse, the apostle tells them, "Such were some of you; but ye are washed, but ye are sanctified, but ye are justified, in the name of the Lord Jesus, and by the Spirit of our God." The people of God have the greater cause of thankfulness, more reason to love God, who hath bestowed such great and unspeakable mercy upon them of his mere sovereign pleasure.

4. *Hence we learn what cause we have to admire the grace of God,* that he should condescend to become bound to us by covenant; that he, who is naturally supreme in his dominion over us, who is our absolute proprietor, and may do with us as he pleases, and is under no obligation to us; that he should, as it were, relinquish his absolute freedom, and should cease to be merely sovereign in his dispensations towards believers, when once they have believed in Christ, and should, for their more abundant consolation, become bound. So that they can challenge salvation of

this Sovereign; they can demand it through Christ, as a debt. And it would be prejudicial to the glory of God's attributes, to deny it to them; it would be contrary to his justice and faithfulness. What wonderful condescension is it in such a Being, thus to become bound to us, worms of the dust, for our consolation! He bound himself by his word, his promise. But he was not satisfied with that; but that we might have stronger consolation still, he hath bound himself by his oath. Heb. 6:13, etc.:

> For when God made promise to Abraham, because he could swear by no greater, he swore by himself; saying, "Surely blessing I will bless thee, and multiplying I will multiply thee." And so, after he had patiently endured, he obtained the promise. For men verily swear by the greater; and an oath for confirmation is to them an end of all strife. Wherein God, willing more abundantly to show unto the heirs of promise the immutability of his counsel, confirmed it by an oath; that by two immutable things, in which it was impossible for God to lie, we might have a strong consolation, who have fled for refuge to lay hold upon the hope set before us. Which hope we have as an anchor of the soul, both sure and steadfast, and which entereth into that within the veil; whither the forerunner is for us entered, even Jesus, made an high priest for ever after the order of Melchisedec.

Let us, therefore, labor to submit to the sovereignty of God. God insists, that his sovereignty be acknowledged by us, and that even in this great matter, a matter which so nearly and infinitely concerns us, as our own eternal salvation. This is the stumbling-block on which thousands fall and perish; and if we go on contending with God about his sovereignty, it will be our eternal ruin. It is absolutely necessary that we should submit to God, as our absolute sovereign, and the sovereign over our souls; as one who may have mercy on whom he will have mercy, and harden whom he will.

5. And lastly. We may make use of this doctrine to guard those who seek salvation from two opposite extremes—presumption and discouragement. Do not presume upon the mercy of God, and so encourage yourself in sin. Many hear that God's mercy is infinite, and therefore think, that if they delay seeking salvation for the present, and seek it hereafter, that God will bestow his grace upon them. But consider, that though God's grace is sufficient, yet he is sovereign, and will use his own pleasure whether he will save you or not. If you put off salvation till hereafter, salvation will not be in your power. It will be as a sovereign God pleases, whether you shall obtain it or not. Seeing, therefore, that in this affair you are so absolutely dependent on God, it is best to follow his direction in seeking it, which is to hear his voice today: "Today if ye will hear his voice, harden not your heart." Beware also of discouragement. Take heed of despairing thoughts, because you are a great sinner, because you have persevered so long in sin, have backslidden, and resisted the Holy Ghost. Remember that, let your case be what it may, and you ever so great a sinner, if you have not committed the sin against the Holy Ghost, God can bestow mercy upon you without the least prejudice to the honor of his holiness, which you have offended, or to the honor of his majesty, which you have insulted, or of his justice, which you have made your enemy, or of his truth, or of any of his attributes. Let you be what sinner you may, God can, if he pleases, greatly glorify himself in your salvation.

Summary

Reference

- Romans 9:18. We observe in the text, God's different dealing with men. He hath mercy on some, and hardeneth others.
- The foundation of his different dealing w/mankind; viz. his sovereign will and pleasure.

Doctrine. God exercises his sovereignty in the eternal salvation of men.

- The sovereignty of God is his absolute, independent right of disposing of all creatures according to his own pleasure.
- The will of God is called his mere pleasure:
    - In opposition to any constraint,
    - In opposition to its being under the will of another,
    - In opposition to any proper obligation.
- What God's sovereignty in the salvation of men implies.
    - God can, without prejudice to the glory of any of his attributes, bestow salvation on any of the children of men, except on those who have committed the sin against the Holy Ghost.
    - God may save any of them without prejudice to the honor of his holiness.
    - God may save any of the children of men without prejudice to the honor of his majesty.

    - God may save any sinner whatsoever consistently with his justice.
    - God can save any sinner whatsoever, without any prejudice to the honor of his truth.
    - God may refuse salvation to any sinner whatsoever, without prejudice to the honor of any of his attributes.
    - God may deny salvation to any natural person without any injury to the honor of his righteousness.
    - God may deny salvation to any unconverted person whatever without any prejudice to the honor of his goodness.
    - It is in no way prejudicial to the honor of God's faithfulness.
- God does actually exercise his sovereignty in men's salvation.
    - In calling one people or nation, and giving them the means of grace, and leaving others without them.
    - In the advantages he bestows upon particular persons.
    - In sometimes bestowing salvation upon the low and mean, and denying it to the wise and great.
    - In bestowing salvation on some who have had few advantages.
    - In calling some to salvation, who have been very heinously wicked, and leaving others, who have been moral and religious persons.
    - In saving some of those who seek salvation, and not others.
- The reasons for this exercise.
    - It is agreeable to God's design in the creation of the universe to exercise every attribute, and thus to manifest the glory of each of them.
    - The more excellent the creature is over whom God is sovereign, and the greater the matter in which he so appears, the more glorious is his sovereignty.

Application

- Hence we learn how absolutely we are dependent on God in this great matter of the eternal salvation of our souls.
- Let us with the greatest humility adore the awful and absolute sovereignty of God.
- Those who are in a state of salvation are to attribute it to sovereign grace alone, and to give all the praise to him, who maketh them to differ from others.

- Hence we learn what cause we have to admire the grace of God, that he should condescend to become bound to us by covenant; etc. Let us, therefore, labor to submit to the sovereignty of God.
- To guard those who seek salvation from two opposite extremes—presumption and discouragement.

Wicked Men Useful in Their Destruction Only

July 1734.

"Son of man, what is the vine tree more than any tree? Or than a branch which is among the trees of the forest? Shall wood be taken thereof to do any work? Or will men take a pin of it to hang any vessel thereon? Behold, it is cast into the fire for fuel; the fire devoureth both the ends of it, and the midst of it, is burnt: Is it meet for any work?"—Ezekiel 15:2–4

The visible church of God is here compared to the vine tree, as is evident by God's own explanation of the allegory, in verses 6, 7, and 8.

> Therefore thus saith the Lord God, "As the vine tree among the trees of the forest, which I have given to the fire for fuel, so will I give the inhabitants of Jerusalem" (etc.).

And it may be understood of mankind in general. We find man often in scripture compared to a vine.

- So in chapter 32 of Deuteronomy: "Their vine is the vine of Sodom, and of the fields of Gomorrah. Their grapes are grapes of gall."

- And Psalm 80:8. "Thou hast brought a vine out of Egypt;" verse 14. "Look down from heaven, behold, and visit this vine."
- And Canticles 2:15. "The foxes that spoil the vines; for our vines have tender grapes."
- Isaiah 5 at the beginning, "My beloved hath a vineyard, and he planted it with the choicest vine."
- Jeremiah 2:21. "I had planted thee a noble vine."
- Hosea 10:1. "Israel is an empty vine."
- So in chapter 15 of John, visible Christians are compared to the branches of a vine.

Man is very fitly represented by the vine. The weakness and dependence of the vine on other things which support it, well represents to us what a poor, feeble, dependent creature man is, and how, if left to himself, he must fall into mischief, and cannot help himself. The visible people of God are fitly compared to a vine, because of the care and cultivation of the husbandman, or vine dresser. The business of husbandmen in the land of Israel was very much in their vineyards, about vines; and the care they exercised to fence them, to defend them, to prune them, to prop them up, and to cultivate them, well represented that merciful care which God exercises towards his visible people; and this latter is often in scripture expressly compared to the former.

In the words now read, is represented:

1. How wholly useless and unprofitable, even beyond other trees, a vine is, in case of unfruitfulness: "What is a vine tree more than any tree, or than a branch which is among the trees of the forest?" i.e. if it does not bear fruit. Men make much more of a vine than of other trees; they take great care of it, to wall it in, to dig about it, to prune it, and the like. It is much more highly esteemed than any one of the trees of the forest; they are despised in comparison with it. And if it bear fruit, it is indeed much preferable to other trees; for the fruit of it yields a noble liquor; as it is said in Jotham's parable, Judges 4:13. "And the vine said unto them, 'Should I leave my wine, which cheereth God and man?' "

But if it bear no fruit, it is more unprofitable than the trees of the forest; for the wood of them is good for timber; but the wood of the vine is fit for no work; as in the text, "Shall wood be taken thereof to do any work? Or will men take a pin of it to hang any vessel thereon?"

2. The only thing for which a vine is useful, in case of barrenness, viz. for fuel: "Behold, it is cast into the fire for fuel." It is wholly consumed; no part of it is worth saving, to make any instrument of it, for any work.

Doctrine

If men bring forth no fruit to God, they are wholly useless, unless in their destruction.

For the proof of this doctrine, I shall show:

- That it is very evident, that there can be but two ways in which man can be useful, viz. either in acting, or in being acted upon, and disposed of.
- That man can no otherwise be useful actively than by bringing forth fruit to God.
- That if he bring not forth fruit to God, there is no other way in which he can be passively useful, but in being destroyed.
- In that way he may be useful without bearing fruit.

I. There are but two ways in which man can be useful, viz. either in *acting* or *being acted upon.*

If man be a useful sort of creature, he must be so either actively or passively: there is no medium. If he be useful to any purpose, he must be so either in acting himself, or else in being disposed of by some other; either in doing something himself to that purpose, or else in having something done upon him by some other to that purpose. What can be more plain, than that if man does nothing himself, and nothing be done with him or upon him by any other, he cannot be any way at all useful? If man does nothing himself to promote the end of his existence, and no other being does anything with him to promote this end, then nothing will be done to promote this end; and so man must be wholly useless. So that there are but two ways in which man can be useful to any purpose, viz. either actively or passively, either in doing something himself, or in being the subject of something done to him.

II. Man cannot be useful *actively*, any otherwise than in bringing forth fruit to God, serving God, and living to his glory.

This is the only way wherein he can be useful in doing; and that for this reason, that the glory of God is the very thing for which man was made, and to which all other ends are subordinate. Man is not an independent being, but he derives his being from another; and therefore hath his end assigned him by that other: and he that gave him his being, made him for the end now mentioned. This was the very design and aim of the

Author of man, this was the work for which he made him, viz. to serve and glorify his Maker.

Other creatures are made for inferior purposes. Inferior creatures were made for inferior purposes. But it is to be observed, that man is the creature that is highest, and nearest to God, of any in this lower world; and therefore his business is with God, although other creatures are made for lower ends. There my be observed a kind of gradation, or gradual ascent, in the order of the different kinds of creatures, from the meanest clod of earth to man, who hath a rational and immortal soul. A plant, an herb, or tree, is superior in nature to a stone or clod, because it hath a vegetable life. The brute creatures are a degree higher still; for they have sensitive life. But man, having a rational soul, is the highest of this lower creation, and is next to God; therefore his business is with God.

Things without life, as earth, water, etc. are subservient to things above them, as the grass, herbs and trees. These vegetables are subservient to that order of creatures which is next above them, the brute creation; they are for food to them. Brute creatures, again, are made for the use and service of the order above them; they are made for the service of mankind. But man being the highest of this lower creation, the next step from him is to God. He therefore is made for the service and glory of God. This is the whole work and business of man; it is his highest end, to which all other ends are subordinate.

If it had not been for this end, there never would have been any such sort of creature as man; there would have been no occasion for it. Other inferior ends may be answered as well, without any such creature as man. There would have been no sort of occasion for making so noble a creature, and endowing him with such faculties, only to enjoy earthly good, to eat, and to drink, and to enjoy sensual things. Brute creatures, without reason, are capable of these things, as well as man; yea, if no higher end be aimed at than to enjoy sensitive good, reason is rather a hindrance than a help. It doth but render man the more capable of afflicting himself with care, and fears of death, and other future evils, and of vexing himself with many anxieties, from which brute creatures are wholly free, and therefore can gratify their senses with less molestation. Besides, reason doth but make men more capable of molesting and impeding one another in the gratification of their senses. If man have no other end to seek but to gratify his senses, reason is nothing but an impediment.

Therefore if man be not made to serve and glorify his Creator, it is wholly to no purpose that such a creature is made. Doubtless then the all wise God, who doth all things in infinite wisdom, hath made man for this end. And this is agreeable to what he hath taught us in many places in the scriptures. This is the great end for which man was made, and for which he was made such a creature as he is, having a body and soul, bodily senses, and rational powers. For this is he placed in such circumstances as he is, and the earth is given him for a possession. For this he hath dominion given him over the rest of the creatures of this world. For this the sun shines on him, and the moon and stars are for signs and seasons to him, and the rain falls on him, and the earth yields him her increase.

All other ends of man are subordinate to this. There are inferior ends for which man was made. Men were made for one another; made for their friends and neighbors, and for the good of the public. But all these inferior ends are designed to be subordinate to the higher end of glorifying God; and therefore man cannot be actively useful, or actively answer any purpose, otherwise than by actively glorifying God, or bringing forth fruit to God. Because:

1. *That is not actively useful which doth not actively answer its end.* That which doth not answer its end is in vain; for that is the meaning of the proposition, that anything is in vain. So that which doth not actively answer its end, is, as to its own activity, in vain.

2. *That is as to its own activity altogether useless which actively answers only subordinate ends, without answering the ultimate end; and that because the ultimate end is the end of subordinate ends.* The notion of a supreme end is, that it is the end of all inferior ends. Subordinate ends are to no purpose, only as they stand related to the highest end. The very notion of a subordinate end is, that it is in order to a further end. Therefore these inferior ends are good for nothing though they be obtained, unless they also obtain their end. Inferior ends are not aimed at for their own sake, but only for the sake of the ultimate end. Therefore he that fails of his great end of all, doth as much altogether fail of his end, and is as much to no purpose, as if he did not obtain his subordinate end.

I will illustrate this by two or three examples. The subordinate end of the underpinning of an house is to support the house; and the subordinate end of the windows is to let in the light. But the ultimate end of the whole is the benefit of the inhabitants. Therefore, if the house be never inhabited, the whole is in vain. The underpinning is in vain, though it be ever so strong and support the building ever so well. The windows also are wholly in vain, though they be ever so large and clear, and though they obtain the subordinate end of letting in the light: they are as much in vain, as if they let in no light.

So the subordinate end of the husbandman in ploughing and sowing, and well manuring his field is, that it may bring forth a crop. But his more ultimate end is, that food may be provided for him and his family. Therefore though his inferior end be obtained, and his field bring forth ever so good a crop, yet if after all it be consumed by fire, or otherwise destroyed, he ploughed and sowed his field as much in vain, as if the seed had never sprung up.

So if man obtain his subordinate ends ever so fully; yet if he altogether fail of his ultimate end, he is wholly an useless creature. Thus if men be very useful in temporal things to their families, or greatly promote the temporal interest of the neighborhood, or of the public; yet if no glory be brought to God by it, they are altogether useless. If men actively bring no glory to God, they are, as to their own activity, altogether useless, how much soever they may promote the benefit of one another. How much soever one part of mankind may subserve another; yet if the end of the whole be not answered, every part is useless.

Thus if the parts of a clock subserve ever so well one to another, mutually to assist each other in their motions; one wheel moving another ever so regularly; yet if the motion never reach the hand or the hammer, it is altogether in vain, as much as if it stood still. As in a clock one wheel moves another, and that another, till at last the motion comes to the hand and hammer, which immediately respect the eye and the ear, otherwise all the motions are in vain; so it is in the world, one man was made to be useful to another, and one part of mankind to another; but the use of the whole is to bring glory to God the maker or else all is in vain; and however a man may serve among his fellow creatures, in a private or public capacity, upon the whole he is in vain.

3. It may perhaps be objected, that a wicked man may, by being serviceable to the public, be useful to many who do bring forth fruit to God, and thus glorify him.

Answer 1. If he be so, he is no further useful than he brings glory to God. It all hath an ultimate respect to that glory that is brought to God, and is useful no further; as the motion of no one wheel of a clock is any further useful, than as it finally respects the right pointing of the hand, and striking of the hammer.

Answer 2. When it is thus, wicked men are useful only accidentally, and not designedly. Although a wicked man may, by being serviceable to good men, do what will be an advantage to them to their bringing forth fruit to God; yet that serviceableness is not what he aims at; this is not his end; he doth not look so far for an ultimate end. And how ever this end be obtained, no thanks are due to him; it is as to him accidental. He is only the occasion, and not the designing cause of it. That fruit which is brought forth to the glory of God, is not brought forth by him, but by others.

The usefulness of such a man, being not designed, is not to be attributed to him as though it were his fruit. He is not useful as a man, or as a rational creature, because he is not so designedly. He is useful as things without life may be. Things without life may be useful to put the godly under advantages to bring forth fruit, as the timber and stones with which his house is built, the wool and flax with which he is clothed; but the fruit which is brought forth to God's glory, cannot be said for all that to be the fruit of these lifeless things, but of the godly man who makes use of them. So it is when wicked men put the godly under advantages to glorify God, as Cyrus, and Artaxerxes, and others have done.

III. If men bring not forth fruit to God, there is no other way in which they can be useful passively, but in being destroyed. They are fit for nothing else.

1. *They are not fit to be suffered to continue always in this world. God suffers them to live for the present, but it is only for a certain season.* They are here in a transitory state. It is not fit that this world should be the constant abode of those who bring forth no fruit to God. It is not fit that the barren tree should be allowed always to stand in the vineyard. The husbandman lets it stand for a while, till he digs about it, dungs it, and proves it to be incurable, or till a convenient time to cut it down come; but it is not fit that such a tree should stand here always. It is not fit that they who bring forth no fruit to God, should be suffered to live always in a world which is so full of the goodness of God, or that his goodness should be spent upon them forever.

This world, though it is fallen, and is under a curse, and is a miserable place to what it once was, yet is full of the streams of divine goodness. But it is not fit that those who bring forth no fruit to God, should always be continued in partaking of these streams. There are these three different states; a state wherein is nothing but good, which is the state of the blessed in heaven; a state wherein is a mixture of good and evil, which is the earthly state ; and a state wherein is nothing but evil, which is the state of eternal destruction and damnation. Now they that bring forth no fruit to God, are not fit for either of the former; it is not fit that they should be continued in the enjoyment of any of the goodness of God.

It is not fit that an unprofitable, unfruitful creature, who will not glorify his Creator, should always live here to devour the fruits of the earth, and consume the fruits of divine bounty; to have the good things of this life, as God's wool and his flax, his corn, and wine, and oil, spent with him in vain. While a man lives in this world, the other creatures of the world are subjected to him. The brute creatures serve him with their labor and with their lives. The sun, moon, and stars, the clouds, fields and trees, all serve him. But it is not fit that these creatures should always be made to serve him, who brings forth no fruit to the Creator. Why should God always keep his creatures in subjection to that man, who will not be subject to him? Why should the creation be always kept in such bondage, as to be subject to wicked men? The creatures are made subject to vanity for a little time; God hath subjected them to wicked men, and given them for their use. This however he would not have done, but as it is only for a little while; and the creatures can bear it through the hope of approaching deliverance; and otherwise it would have been intolerable. Romans 8:20. "For the creature was made subject to vanity, not willingly, but by reason of him who hath subjected the same in hope."

The creature doth, as it were, groan by reason of this subjection to wicked men, although it be but for a while. Romans 8:22. "For we know that the whole creation groaneth, and travaileth in pain together until now." Therefore surely it would be no way fit that wicked men, who do no good, and bring forth no fruit to God, should live here always, to have the various creatures subservient to them, as they are now. The earth can scarcely bear wicked men during that short time for which they stay here, but is ready to spew thee out. It is no way fit, therefore, that it should be forced to bear them always.

Men who bring forth no fruit to God are cumberers of the ground. Luke 8:7: "And it is not meet that they should be suffered to cumber the ground always." God cannot be glorified in this way of disposing of unfruitful persons. If such men should be suffered to live always in such a state as this, it would be so far from being to the glory of God, that it would be to the disparagement of the wisdom of God, to continue them in a state so unsuitable for them, forever spending the fruits of his bounty in vain upon them. It would also be a disparagement to his justice; for this is a world where, "all things come alike to all, and there is one event to the righteous and to the wicked" [Ecc. 9:2]. If there were no other state but this for wicked men to be in, justice could not possibly take place. It would also reflect upon the holiness of God. Forever to uphold this world for an habitation of such persons, and forever to continue the communications of his bounty and goodness to them, would appear as though he were disposed to countenance and encourage sin and wickedness.

2. If men do not bring forth fruit to God, they are not fit to be disposed of in heaven. Heaven, above all others, is the most improper place for them. Everything appertaining to that state is unsuitable for them. The company is most unsuitable. The original inhabitants of that world are the angels. But what a disagreeable union would that be, to unite wicked men and angels in the same society? The employments of that world are unsuitable. The employments are serving and glorifying God. How unsuitable then would it be to plant barren trees in that heavenly paradise, trees that would bring forth no fruit to the divine glory? The enjoyments of heaven are unsuitable. The enjoyments are holy and spiritual enjoyments, the happiness of beholding the glory of God, and praising his name, and the like. But these enjoyments are as unsuitable as can be to the carnal earthly minds of wicked men. They would be no enjoyments to them; but on the contrary would be most disagreeable, and what they cannot relish, but entirely nauseate.

The design of heaven is unsuitable to them. The design of God in making heaven was, that it might be a place of holy habitation, for the reward of the righteous, and not an habitation for wicked men. It would greatly reflect on the wisdom of God to dispose of wicked men there; for it would be the greatest confusion. But God is not the author of confusion, 1 Corrinthians 14:33. It would be contrary to the holiness of God, to take wicked men so near to himself into his glorious presence, to dwell forever in that part of the creation which is, as it were, his own palace, and to sit at his table. We read in Psalm 5:4. "Thou art not a God that hath pleasure in wickedness, neither shall evil dwell with thee." Therefore it would doubtless be impossible that the end of the existence of wicked men should be in any wise answered by the placing of them in heaven.

IV. Men who bring forth no fruit to God, yet in suffering destruction may be useful.

Although they be not useful actively, or by anything which they do; yet they may be useful in what they may suffer; just as a barren tree, which is no way useful standing in the vineyard, yet may be good fuel, and be very useful in the fire. God can find use for the most wicked men; he hath his use for vessels of wrath as well as for vessels of mercy; as in an house there is use for vessels unto dishonor, as well as for vessels unto honor. 2 Timothy 2:20. "In a great house there are not only vessels of gold, and of silver, but also of wood and of earth; and some to honor, and some to dishonor." Proverbs 16:4. "The Lord hath made all things for himself; yea, even the wicked for the day of evil." I shall briefly take notice of what ends God accomplishes by it.

1. *Unfruitful persons are of use in their destruction for the glory of God's justice.* It was the will of God to glorify his justice, as well as his mercy, on his creatures. The vindictive justice of God is a glorious attribute, as well as his mercy; and the glory of this attribute appears in the everlasting destruction and ruin of the barren and unfruitful.

The glory of divine justice in the perdition of ungodly men appears wonderful and glorious in the eyes of the saints and angels in heaven. Hence we have an account, that they sing praises to God, and extol his justice at the sight of the awful judgments which he inflicts on wicked men. Revelation 16:5, "Thou art righteous, O Lord, which art and wast, and art to come, because thou hast judged thus; for they have shed the blood of saints and prophets, and thou hast given them blood to drink; for they are worthy:" And Revelation 19:1, 2:

> And after these things I heard a great voice, saying, "Alleluia: Salvation, and glory, and honor, and power, unto the Lord our God; for true and righteous are his judgments, for he hath judged the great whore, which did corrupt the earth with her fornication, and hath avenged the blood of his servants at her hand."

2. *Unfruitful persons in their destruction are of use for God to glorify his majesty upon them.* The awful majesty of God remarkably appears in those dreadful and amazing punishments which he inflicts on those who rise up against him, and contemn him. A sense of the majesty of an earthly prince is supported very much by a sense of its being a dreadful thing to affront him. God glorifies his own majesty in the destruction of wicked men; and herein he appears infinitely great, in that it appears to be an infinitely dreadful thing to offend him. How awful doth the majesty of God appear in the dreadfulness of his anger! This we may learn to be one end of the damnation of the wicked, from Romans 9:22.

> What if God, willing to show his wrath, and to make his power known, endured with much long suffering the vessels of wrath fitted to destruction?

It is often spoken of God, that he is a terrible God. It is a part of the majesty and glory of God, that he is a terrible God. God tells Pharaoh, that for this cause he raised him up, that he might show his power in him, and that his name might be declared through all the earth, in his destruction. Exodus 9:15, 16; and again, chapter 14:17: "I will get me [myself] honor [through my vengeance] upon Pharaoh, and upon all his host, upon his chariots, and upon his horsemen."

3. *The destruction of the unfruitful is of use, to give the saints a greater sense of their happiness, and of God's grace to them.* The wicked will be destroyed and tormented in the view of the saints, and other inhabitants of heaven. This we are taught in Revelation 14:10.

> The same shall drink of the wine of the wrath of God, which is poured out without mixture, into the cup of his indignation; and he shall be tormented with fire and brimstone, in the presence of the holy angels, and in the presence of the Lamb.

And in Isaiah 56:24:

> And they shall go forth and look upon the carcasses of the men that have transgressed against me. For their worm shall not die, neither shall their fire be quenched, and they shall be an abhorring unto all flesh.

When the saints in heaven shall look upon the damned in Hell, it will serve to give them a greater sense of their own happiness, seeing how vastly different their case is from their own. The view of the doleful condition of the damned will make them the more prize their own blessedness. When they shall see how dreadful the anger of God is, it will make them the more prize his love. They will rejoice so much the more that they are not the objects of God's anger, but of his favor; that they are not the subjects of his dreadful wrath, but are treated as his children, are taken near to him, to dwell in the everlasting embraces of his love.

When they shall see the misery of the damned, it will give them a greater sense of the distinguishing grace and love of God to them, that God should from all eternity set his love on them, and make so great a difference between them and others who are of the same species with them, are no worse by nature than they, and have deserved no worse of God than they. When they shall look upon the misery of the damned, and consider how different their own state is from theirs, and that it is only free and sovereign grace that makes the difference, what a great sense will this give them of the wonderful grace of God to them! And how will it heighten their praises! With how much greater admiration and exultation of soul will they sing of the free and sovereign grace of God to them!

When they shall look upon the damned, and see their misery, how will heaven ring with the praises of God's justice towards the wicked, and his grace towards the saints! And with how much greater enlargement of heart will they praise Jesus Christ their Redeemer, that ever he was pleased to set his love upon them, his dying love! And that he should so distinguish them as to spill his blood, and make his soul an offering, to redeem them from that so great misery, and to bring them to such exceeding happiness!

With what love and ecstasy will they sing that song in Revelation 5:9,10.

> Thou art worthy: For thou wast slain, and hast redeemed us to God by thy blood, out of every tongue, and kindred, and people, and nation; and hast made us unto our God kings and priests.

One end which the apostle mentions, why God appointed vessels of wrath, is the more to make known the wonderfulness of his mercy towards the saints. In Romans 9:22, 23, there are two ends mentioned:

> What if God, willing to show his wrath, and to make his power known, endured with much long suffering the vessels of wrath fitted to destruction?

That is one end, then another is mentioned immediately after:

> And that he might make known the riches of his glory on the vessels of mercy, which he had afore prepared unto glory.

Application

I. Hence we may learn, how just and righteous God is in the destruction of those who bring forth no fruit to God.

Seeing there is no other way in which they can be useful, or in which the end of their being can be obtained, certainly it is most just that God should thus dispose of them. Why should God be frustrated of his end through their perverseness? If men will not do the work for which he hath made and fitted them; if they, through a spirit of opposition and rebellion against God, refuse; yet why should God suffer himself to be disappointed of his end in making them? It doth not become the infinite greatness and majesty of God, to suffer himself to be disappointed and frustrated by the wickedness and perverseness of sinful worms of the dust. If God should suffer this, it would seem to argue, either a want of wisdom in God to fix upon a good end, or a want of power to accomplish it.

God made all men that they might be useful; and if they will not be useful in their conduct and actions, how just is it that God should make them useful in their sufferings! God made all men for his own glory; and if they, contrary to the revealed will of God, refuse to glorify him actively and willingly, how just is it that God should glorify himself upon them in what he doth with them!

It hath been shown, that there is no other way wherein this can be done, but by their destruction. Surely, therefore, it must be just and righteous that God should destroy them.

Men are under no natural necessity of being put to this use of glorifying God in their sufferings. God gives them opportunity of glorifying him in doing, in bringing forth fruit, puts them under advantages for it, and uses many means to bring them to it. But if they will not be useful this way, it is very just that God should make them useful in the only remaining way in which they can be useful, viz. in their destruction. God is not forward to put them to this use. He tells us, that he hath "no pleasure in the death of the wicked; but that the wicked turn from his way, and live;" Ezekiel 33:11. God represents the destruction of sinners as a work to which he is backward; yet it is meet that they should be destroyed, rather than that they should be suffered to frustrate God of the end of their being. Who can blame the husbandman for cutting down and burning a barren tree, after he hath digged about it, and dunged it, and used all proper means to make it fruitful?

Let those among us consider this, who have lived all their lives hitherto unprofitably, and never have brought forth any fruit to God's glory, notwithstanding all the means that have been used with them. Consider how just it would be if God should utterly destroy you, and glorify himself upon you in that way; and what a wonder of patience it is, that God hath not done it before now.

II. This subject ought to put you upon examining yourselves, whether you be not wholly useless creatures.

You have now heard, that those who bring forth no fruit to God, are, as to any good they do, wholly useless. Inquire, therefore, whether you have ever in your lives brought forth any fruit to God. Have you ever done anything from a gracious respect to God, or out of love to God? Seeking only your worldly interest, you do not bring forth fruit to God. It is not bringing forth fruit to God, for you to come to public worship on the Sabbath, to pray in your families, and other such like things, merely in compliance with the general custom. It is not to bring forth fruit to God, that you be sober, moral and religious, only to be seen of men, or out of respect to your own credit and honor. How is that for God which is only for the sake of custom, or the esteem of men, of for the fear of Hell?

What thanks are due to you for not loving your own misery, and for being willing to take some pains to escape burning in Hell to all eternity? There is ne'er a devil in Hell but would gladly do the same. Hosea 10:1. "Israel is an empty vine; he bringeth forth fruit unto himself."

There is no fruit brought forth to God, where there is nothing done in any wise from love to God, or from any true respect to him. God looketh at the heart. He doth not stand in need of our services, neither is he benefitted by anything that we can do. He doth not receive anything of us, because it benefits him, but only as a suitable testimony of our love and respect to him. This is the fruit that he seeks. Men themselves will not accept of those shows of friendship, which they think are hypocritical, and come not from the heart. How much less should God, who searcheth the hearts and trieth the reins of the children of men! John 4:23. "God is a spirit, and they that worship him must worship him in spirit and in truth."
Inquire, therefore, whether you ever in your lives did the least thing out of love to God. Have you not done all for yourselves? Zechariah 7:5, 6:

> When ye fasted and mourned in the fifth and seventh month, even those seventy years, did ye at all fast unto me, even unto me? And when ye did eat, and when ye did drink, did ye not eat for yourselves, and drink for yourselves?

III. Another use of this subject may be of conviction and humiliation to those who never have brought forth any fruit to God.

If, upon examination, you find that you have never in all your lives done anything out of a true respect to God, then it hath been demonstrated, that, as to anything which you do, you are altogether useless creatures. And consider, what a shameful thing it is for such rational beings as you are, and placed under such advantages for usefulness, yet to be wholly useless, and to live in the world to no purpose!

We esteem it a very mean character in any person, that he is a worthless, insignificant person; and to be called so is taken as a great reproach. But consider seriously, whether you can clear yourselves of this character. Set reason to work; can you rationally suppose, that you do in any measure answer the end for which God gave you your being, and made you of a nature superior to the beasts? But that you may be sensible what cause you have to be ashamed of your unprofitableness, consider the following things.

1. *How much God hath bestowed upon you, in the endowments of your nature.* God hath made you rational, intelligent creatures, hath endowed you with noble powers, those endowments wherein the natural image of God consists. You are vastly exalted in your nature above other kinds of creatures here below. You are capable of a thousand times as much as any of the brute creatures. He hath given you a power of understanding, which is capable of vastly extending itself, of looking back to the beginning of time, and of considering what was before the world was, and of looking forward beyond the end of time. It is capable of extending beyond the utmost limits of the universe; and is a faculty whereby you are akin to angels, and are capable even of knowing God, of contemplating the divine Being, and his glorious perfections, manifested in his works and in his word. You have souls capable of being the habitation of the Holy Spirit of God, and his divine grace. You are capable of the noble employments of angels.

How lamentable and shameful it is, that such a creature should be altogether useless, and live in vain! How lamentable that such a noble and excellent piece of divine workmanship should fail of its end, and be to no purpose! Was it ever worth while for God to make you such a creature, with such a noble nature, and so much above other kinds of creatures, only to eat, and drink, and gratify your sensual appetites? How lamentable and shameful to you, that such a noble tree should be more useless than any tree of the forest; that man, whom God hath thus set in honor, should make himself more worthless than the beasts that perish!

2. *How much God hath done for you in the creation of the world.* He made the earth, and seas, and all the fullness of them, for the use of man, and hath given them to him. Psalm 115:16. "The earth hath he given to the children of men." He made the vast variety of creatures for man's use and service. Genesis 1:28. "Have dominion over the fish of the sea, and over the fowl of the air, and over every living thing that moveth upon the earth." For the same purpose he made all the plants, and herbs, and trees of the field. Genesis 1:29:

> I have given you every herb bearing seed, which is upon the face of all the earth, and every tree, in the which is the fruit of a tree, yielding seed; to you it shall be for meat.

He made the sun in the heavens, that glorious luminary, that wonderful globe of light, to give light to man, and to constitute the difference between day and night. He also made the moon, and the vast multitude of stars, for the use of man, to be to him for signs and seasons.

What great provision hath God made for man! What a vast variety of good things for food, and otherwise to be for his convenience, to put him under advantages to be useful! How lamentable is it, that after all these things he should be an useless creature in the world!

3. *How much is done for you in the course of God's common providence!* Consider how nature is continually laboring for you. The sun is, as it were, in a ferment for mankind, unweariedly running his course from year to year, and from day to day, and spending his rays upon man, to put him under advantage to be useful; every day giving him light that he may have opportunity to behold the glorious wisdom of God, and to see and serve God. The winds and clouds are continually laboring for you, and the waters are going in a constant circulation, ascending in the air from the seas, descending in rain, gathering in streams and rivers, returning to the sea, and again ascending and descending, for you. The earth is continually laboring to bring forth her fruit for your support. The trees of the field are laboring and spending their strength for you. And how many of the poor brute creatures are continually laboring for you, and spending their strength for you! How much of the earth is spent upon you! How many of God's creatures are devoured by you! How many of the lives of the living creatures of God are destroyed for your sake, for your support and comfort!

Now, how lamentable will it be, if, after all, you be altogether useless, and live to no purpose! What mere cumberers of the ground will you be, agreeably to Luke 13:7 [the parable of the barren fig tree]. Nature, which thus continually labors for you, will be burdened with you. This seems to be what the apostle means, Romans 8:20–22, where he tells us, that the creation is made subject to vanity, and brought into the bondage of corruption; and that the whole creation groans, and travails in pain, under this bondage.

4. *How much is done for you in the use of the means of grace.* How much hath God done to provide you with suitable means and advantages for usefulness! How many prophets hath God sent into the world, in different ages, inspiring them with his Holy Spirit, and enabling them to work many miracles to confirm their word, whereby you now have the written word of God to instruct you!

How great a thing hath God done for you, to give you opportunity and advantage to be useful, in that he hath sent his own Son into the world! He who is really and truly God, united himself to the human nature, and became a man, to be a prophet and teacher to you and other sinners. Yea, he laid down his life to make atonement for sin, that you might have encouragement to serve God with hopes of acceptance.

How many ordinances have been instituted for you! How much of the labor of the ministers of God hath been spent upon you! Is not that true concerning you which is written in Isaiah 5 at the beginning, concerning the vineyard planted in a very fruitful hill, and fenced and cultivated with peculiar care and pains, which yet proved unfruitful? How much hath the dresser of the vineyard digged about the barren tree, and dunged it, and yet it remains barren!

Consider what a shame it is that you should live in vain, when all the other creatures, that are inferior to you, do glorify their Creator, according to their nature. You who are so highly exalted in the world, are more useless than the brute creation; yea, than the meanest worms, or things without life, as earth and stones. For they all do answer their end, in the way in which nature hath fitted them for it; none of them fail of it. They are all useful in their places, all render their proper tribute of praise to their Creator; while you are mere nuisances in the creation, and burdens to the earth; as any tree of the forest is more useful than the vine, if it bear not fruit.

IV. Let me, in a farther application of this doctrine, exhort you by all means to bring forth fruit to God.

Let it be your constant endeavor to be in this way actively useful in the world. Here consider three things.

1. *What an honor it will be to such poor creatures as you are, to bring forth fruit to the divine glory.* What is such a poor worm as man, that he should be enabled to bring forth any fruit to God! It is the greatest honor of the nature of man, that God hath given him a capacity of glorifying the great Creator. It is what no other creature in this lower world can do, in the same manner as man. There is no creature in the visible world that is capable of actively glorifying God, but man.

2. *In bringing forth fruit to God, you will be so profitable to none as to yourselves; you cannot thereby be profitable to God.* Job 22:2: "Can a man be profitable to God?" You may thereby be profitable to your fellow creatures; yet not so much as to yourselves. The fruit which you bring forth to God will be a greater benefit to yourselves than to anyone living. You will be more useful to yourselves than to anyone else.

Although you are under a natural obligation to bring forth fruit to God, yet God doth not require it of you without a reward. He will richly reward you for it. In requiring you to bring forth fruit to him, he doth but require you to bring forth fruit to your own happiness. You will taste the sweetness of your own fruit. It will be most profitable for you in this world to bring forth fruit to God; it will be exceedingly to your benefit while here. It will be pleasant to you to lead a fruitful and holy life; the pleasure will be beyond the labor. Beside this, God hath promised to such a life everlasting rewards, unspeakable, infinite benefits. So that by it you will infinitely advance your own interest.

3. *If you remain thus unprofitable, and be not actively useful, surely God will obtain his end of you, in your destruction.* He will say concerning the barren tree, "Cut it down, why cumbereth it the ground?" Christ, in John 15:6, tells us, "if a man abide not in me, he is cast forth as a branch, and is withered; and men gather them, and cast them into the fire, and they are burned." This is spoken of the barren branches in the vine. How would you yourselves do in such a case with a barren tree in an orchard, or with weeds and tares in your fields? Doubtless, it were in your power, you would utterly destroy them.

God will have his end; he will accomplish it. Though all men and devils unite their endeavors, they cannot frustrate God in anything; and "though hand join in hand, the wicked shall not be unpunished;" Proverbs 11:1. God hath sworn by his great name, that he will have his glory of men, whether they will actively glorify him or no. Numbers 14:21–23.

> But as truly as I live, all the earth shall be filled with the glory of the Lord. Because all those men which have seen my glory, and my miracles which I did in Egypt and in the wilderness, and have tempted me now these ten times, and have not hearkened to my voice; surely they shall not see the land which I sware unto their fathers, neither shall any of them that provoked me, see it.

"The ax lieth at the root of the trees; and every tree which bringeth not forth good fruit, is hewn down, and cast into the fire;" Matthew 3:10. The end of those men who bring forth nothing but briers and thorns is to be burned, as in Hebrews 6:7, 8:

> For the earth which drinketh in the rain that cometh oft upon it, and bringeth forth herbs meet for them by whom it is dressed, receiveth blessing from God: But that which beareth thorns and briers, is rejected, and is nigh unto cursing; whose end is to be burned.

So we read of the tares, Matthew 13:30:

> Let both grow together until the harvest ; and in the time of harvest I will say to the reapers, "Gather ye together first the tares, and bind them in bundles to burn them;"

and in verses 40–42,

> As therefore the tares are gathered and burned in the fire, so shall it be at the end of the world. The Son of man shall send forth his angels, and they shall gather out of his kingdom all things that offend, and them which do iniquity, and shall cast them into a furnace of fire: There shall be wailing and gnashing of teeth.

So it is said of the chaff, Matthew 3:12. "Whose fan is in his hand, and he will thoroughly purge his floor, and gather his wheat into the garner; but he will burn up the chaff with unquenchable fire."

If you continue not to bring forth any fruit to the divine glory, as you have hitherto done, Hell will be the only fit place for you. It is a place prepared on purpose to be a receptacle of such persons. In Hell, nature ceases to labor any more for sinners: The sun doth not run his course to shine upon them, the earth doth not bring forth her fruit to be consumed upon them there. There they will have no opportunity to consume the fruits of divine goodness on their lusts. In Hell they can prejudice or encumber nothing, upon which God sets any value. There the faithful servants and ministers of God will no longer spend their strength in vain upon them. When the barren tree is in the fire, the servants of the husbandman are freed from any further labor or toil in digging about it, and manuring it.

In Hell they will no more have opportunity to clog and discourage the flourishing of religion, and to destroy much good, as they often do in this world. In Hell they will no more have opportunity to corrupt others by their ill example. In Hell they will no more have it in their power to offend the godly; they may hurt and torment one another; but the godly will be out of their reach. In Hell there will be no ordinances, no Sabbaths, no sacraments, no sacred things, for them to profane and defile by their careless and hypocritical attendance.

Hell, therefore, if you remain unfruitful and cumberers of the ground, will be the fittest place for you, and there you will surely have your portion assigned you. There God will get himself honor upon you; there he will magnify himself in your ruin, in the presence of the holy angels, and in the presence of the Lamb; and will be praised upon that account by the saints, at the day of judgment; and by all the host of heaven throughout everlasting ages.

A Divine and Supernatural Light

Immediately Imparted to the Soul by the Spirit of God, Shown to be Both Scriptural and Rational Doctrine

This sermon was preached at Northampton in the year 1734, and excited uncommon interest in the hearers, so that, at their request, it was published.

"And Jesus answered and said unto him, 'Blessed art thou, Simon Barjona: for flesh and blood hath not revealed it unto thee, but my Father which is in heaven.' "—Matthew 16:17

Christ says these words to Peter upon occasion of his professing his faith in him as the Son of God. Our Lord was inquiring of his disciples, who men said he was; not that he needed to be informed, but only to introduce and give occasion to what follows. They answer, that some said he was John the Baptist, and some Elias, and others Jeremias, or one of the prophets. When they had thus given an account who others said he was, Christ asks them, who they said he was? Simon Peter, whom we find always zealous and forward, was the first to answer: he readily replied to the question, "Thou art Christ, the Son of the living God."

Upon this occasion, Christ says as he does *to* him, and *of* him in the text: in which we may observe,

- *That Peter is pronounced blessed on this account.*

  Blessed art thou—thou art a happy man, that thou art not ignorant of this, that I am *Christ, the Son of the living God*. Thou art distinguishingly happy. Others are blinded, and have dark and deluded apprehensions, as you have now given an account, some thinking that I am Elias, and some that I am Jeremias, and some one thing, and some another; but none of them thinking right, all of them misled. Happy art thou, that art so distinguished as to know the truth in this matter.

- *The evidence of this his happiness declared; viz., that God, and he only, had revealed it to him.* This is an evidence of his being *blessed.*

  First, as it shows how peculiarly favored he was of God above others; q.d.:

  How highly favored art thou, that others that are wise and great men, the scribes, Pharisees, and rulers, and the nation in general, are left in darkness, to follow their own misguided apprehensions; and that thou shouldst be singled out, as it were, by name, that my Heavenly Father should thus set his love, on *thee, Simon Bar-jona*. This argues thee *blessed*, that thou shouldst thus be the object of God's distinguishing love.

  Secondly, it evidences his blessedness also, as it intimates that this knowledge is above any that flesh and blood can reveal.

  This is such knowledge as only my *Father which is in heaven* can give: it is too high and excellent to be communicated by such means as other knowledge is. Thou art *blessed*, that thou knowest that which God alone can teach thee."

The original of this knowledge is here declared, both negatively and positively. *Positively*, as God is here declared the author of it. *Negatively*, as it is declared, that *flesh and blood* had *not revealed it*. God is the author of all knowledge and understanding whatsoever. He is the author of the knowledge that is obtained by human learning: he is the author of all moral prudence, and of the knowledge and skill that men have in their secular business. Thus it is said of all in Israel that were *wise-hearted*, and skilled in embroidering, that God had *filled* them *with the spirit of wisdom*, Exodus 28:3.

God is the author of such knowledge; but yet not so but that *flesh and blood reveals it. Mortal men are capable of imparting the knowledge of human arts and sciences, and skill in temporal affairs. God is the author of such knowledge by those means: flesh and blood* is employed as the *mediate* or *second* cause of it; he conveys it by the power and influence of natural means. But this spiritual knowledge, spoken of in the text, is what God is the author of, and none else: he *reveals it*, and *flesh and blood reveals it not*. He imparts this knowledge immediately, not making use of any intermediate natural causes, as he does in other knowledge.

What had passed in the preceding discourse naturally occasioned Christ to observe this; because the disciples had been telling how others did not know him, but were generally mistaken about him, and divided and confounded in their opinions of him: but Peter had declared his assured faith, that he was the *Son of God*. Now it was natural to observe, how it was not *flesh and blood* that had *revealed it to him*, but God: for if this knowledge were dependent on natural causes or means, how came it to pass that they, a company of poor fishermen, illiterate men, and persons of low education, attained to the knowledge of the truth; while the Scribes and Pharisees, men of vastly higher advantages, and greater knowledge and sagacity in other matters, remained in ignorance? This could be owing only to the gracious distinguishing influence and revelation of the Spirit of God. Hence, what I would make the subject of my present discourse from these words, is this

Doctrine

That there is such a thing as a spiritual and divine light immediately imparted to the soul by God, of a different nature from any that is obtained by natural means. And on this subject I would,

I. Show what this divine light is.

II. Show how it is given immediately by God, and not obtained by natural means.

III. Show the truth of the doctrine.

IV. And then conclude with a brief improvement.

I. I would show what this spiritual and divine light is. And in order to do it, would show,

1. *In a few things, what it is not*. And here,

First, those convictions that natural men may have of their sin and misery, is not this spiritual and divine light. Men in a natural condition may have convictions of the guilt that lies upon them, and of the anger of God, and their danger of divine vengeance. Such convictions are from light or sensibleness of truth. That some sinners have a greater conviction of their guilt and misery than others, is because some have more light, or more of an apprehension of truth than others. And this light and conviction may be from the Spirit of God; the Spirit convinces men of sin: but yet nature is much more concerned in it than in the communication of that spiritual and divine light that is spoken of in the doctrine; it is from the Spirit of God only as assisting natural principles, and not as infusing any new principles. Common grace differs from special, in that it influences only by assisting of nature; and not by imparting grace, or bestowing anything above nature. The light that is obtained is wholly natural, or of no superior kind to what mere nature attains to, though more of that kind be obtained than would be obtained if men were left wholly to themselves: or, in other words, common grace only assists the faculties of the soul to do that more fully which they do by nature, as natural conscience or reason will, by mere nature, make a man sensible of guilt, and will accuse and condemn him when he has done amiss. Conscience is a principle natural to men; and the work that it doth naturally, or of itself, is to give an apprehension of right and wrong, and to suggest to the mind the relation that there is between right and wrong, and a retribution. The Spirit of God, in those convictions which unregenerate men sometimes have, assists conscience to do this work in a further degree than it would do if they were left to themselves: he helps it against those things that tend to stupefy it, and obstruct its exercise. But in the renewing and sanctifying work of the Holy Ghost, those things are wrought in the soul that are above nature, and of which there is nothing of the like kind in the soul by nature; and they are caused to exist in the soul habitually, and according to such a stated constitution or law that lays such a foundation for exercises in a continued course, as is called a principle of nature. Not only are remaining principles assisted to do their work more freely and fully, but those principles are restored that were utterly destroyed by the fall; and the mind thence forward habitually exerts those acts that the dominion of sin had made it as wholly destitute of, as a dead body is of vital acts.

The Spirit of God acts in a very different manner in the one case, from what he doth in the other. He may indeed act upon the mind of a natural man, but he acts in the mind of a saint as an indwelling vital principle. He acts upon the mind of an unregenerate person as an extrinsic, occasional agent; for in acting upon them, he doth not unite himself to them; for notwithstanding all his influences that they may be the subjects of, they are still sensual, having not the Spirit (Jude 19). But he unites himself with the mind of a saint, takes him for his temple, and actuates and influences him as a new supernatural principle of life and action. There is this difference, that the Spirit of God, in acting in the soul of a godly man, exerts and communicates himself there in his own proper nature. Holiness is the proper nature of the Spirit of God. The Holy Spirit operates in the minds of the godly, by uniting himself to them, and living in them, and exerting his own nature in the exercise of their faculties. The Spirit of God may act upon a creature, and yet not in acting communicate himself. The Spirit of God may act upon inanimate creatures; as, "the Spirit moved upon the face of the waters," in the beginning of the creation; so the Spirit of God may act upon the minds of men many ways, and communicate himself no more than when he acts upon an inanimate creature. For instance, he may excite thoughts in them, may assist their natural reason and understanding, or may assist other natural principles, and this without any union with the soul, but may act, as it were, as upon an external object. But as he acts in his holy influences and spiritual operations, he acts in a way of peculiar communication of himself; so that the subject is thence denominated "spiritual."

Secondly, this spiritual and divine light does not consist in any impression made upon the imagination. It is no impression upon the mind, as though one saw anything with the bodily eyes: it is no imagination or idea of an outward light or glory, or any beauty of form or countenance, or a visible luster or brightness of any object. The imagination may be strongly impressed with such things; but this is not spiritual light. Indeed, when the mind has a lively discovery of spiritual things, and is greatly affected by the power of divine light, it may, and probably very commonly doth, much affect the imagination; so that impressions of an outward beauty or brightness may accompany those spiritual discoveries. But spiritual light is not that impression upon the imagination, but an exceeding different thing from it. Natural men may have lively impressions on their imaginations; and we cannot determine but the devil, who transforms himself into an angel of light, may cause imaginations of an outward beauty, or visible glory, and of sounds and speeches, and other such things; but these are things of a vastly inferior nature to spiritual light.

Thirdly, this spiritual light is not the suggesting of any new truths or propositions not contained in the word of God. This suggesting of new truths or doctrines to the mind, independent of any antecedent revelation of those propositions, either in word or writing, is inspiration; such as the prophets and apostles had, and such as some enthusiasts pretend to. But this spiritual light that I am speaking of, is quite a different thing from inspiration: it reveals no new doctrine, it suggests no new proposition to the mind, it teaches no new thing of God, or Christ, or another world, not taught in the Bible, but only gives a due apprehension of those things that are taught in the word of God.

Fourthly, it is not every affecting view that men have of the things of religion that is this spiritual and divine light. Men by mere principles of nature are capable of being affected with things that have a special relation to religion as well as other things. A person by mere nature, for instance, may be liable to be affected with the story of Jesus Christ, and the sufferings he underwent, as well as by any other tragical story: he may be the more affected with it from the interest he conceives mankind to have in it. Yea, he may be affected with it without believing it; as well as a man may be affected with what he reads in a romance, or sees acted in a stage play. He may be affected with a lively and eloquent description of many pleasant things that attend the state of the blessed in heaven, as well as his imagination be entertained by a romantic description of the pleasantness of fairy land, or the like. And that common belief of the truth of the things of religion, that persons may have from education or otherwise, may help forward their affection. We read in Scripture of many that were greatly affected with things of a religious nature, who yet are there represented as wholly graceless, and many of them very ill men. A person therefore may have affecting views of the things of religion, and yet be very destitute of spiritual light. Flesh and blood may be the author of this: one man may give another an affecting view of divine things with but common assistance: but God alone can give a spiritual discovery of them.

2. *But I proceed to show, positively what this spiritual and divine light* is.

And it may be thus described: a true sense of the divine excellency of the things revealed in the word of God, and a conviction of the truth and reality of them thence arising. This spiritual light primarily consists in the former of these, viz., a real sense and apprehension of the divine excellency of things revealed in the word of God. A spiritual and saving conviction of the truth and reality of these things arises from such a sight of their divine excellency and glory; so that this conviction of their truth is an effect and natural consequence of this sight of their divine glory. There is therefore in this spiritual light:

First, a true sense of the divine and superlative excellency of the things of religion; a real sense of the excellency of God and Jesus Christ, and of the work of redemption, and the ways and works of God revealed in the gospel. There is a divine and superlative glory in these things; an excellency that is of a vastly higher kind, and more sublime nature than in other things; a glory greatly distinguishing them from all that is earthly and temporal. He that is spiritually enlightened truly apprehends and sees it, or has a sense of it. He does not merely rationally believe that God is glorious, but he has a sense of the gloriousness of God in his heart. There is not only a rational belief that God is holy, and that holiness is a good thing, but there is a sense of the loveliness of God's holiness. There is not only a speculatively judging that God is gracious, but a sense how amiable God is upon that account, or a sense of the beauty of this divine attribute.

There is a twofold understanding or knowledge of good that God has made the mind of man capable of. The first, that which is merely speculative and notional; as when a person only speculatively judges that anything is, which, by the agreement of mankind, is called good or excellent, viz., that which is most to general advantage, and between which and a reward there is a suitableness, and the like. And the other is, that which consists in the sense of the heart: as when there is a sense of the beauty, amiableness, or sweetness of a thing; so that the heart is sensible of pleasure and delight in the presence of the idea of it. In the former is exercised merely the speculative faculty, or the understanding, strictly so called, or as spoken of in distinction from the will or disposition of the soul. In the latter, the will, or inclination, or heart, are mainly concerned.

Thus there is a difference between having an *opinion*, that God is holy and gracious, and having a *sense* of the loveliness and beauty of that holiness and grace. There is a difference between having a rational judgment that honey is sweet, and having a sense of its sweetness. A man may have the former, that knows not how honey tastes; but a man cannot have the latter unless he has an idea of the taste of honey in his mind. So there is a difference between believing that a person is beautiful, and having a sense of his beauty. The former may be obtained by hearsay, but the latter only by seeing the countenance. There is a wide difference between mere speculative rational judging anything to be excellent, and having a sense of its sweetness and beauty. The former rests only in the head, speculation only is concerned in it; but the heart is concerned in the latter. When the heart is sensible of the beauty and amiableness of a thing, it necessarily feels pleasure in the apprehension. It is implied in a person's being heartily sensible of the loveliness of a thing, that the idea of it is sweet and pleasant to his soul; which is a far different thing from having a rational opinion that it is excellent.

Secondly, there arises from this sense of divine excellency of things contained in the word of God, a conviction of the truth and reality of them; and that either directly or indirectly.

Indirectly, and that two ways.

- *First, as the prejudices that are in the heart, against the truth of divine things, are hereby removed; so the mind becomes susceptive to the due force of rational arguments for their truth.* The mind of man is naturally full of prejudices against the truth of divine things: it is full of enmity against the doctrines of the gospel; which is a disadvantage to those arguments that prove their truth, and causes them to lose their force upon the mind. But when a person has discovered to him the divine excellency of Christian doctrines, this destroys the enmity, removes those prejudices, and sanctifies the reason, and causes it to lie open to the force of arguments for their truth.

    Hence was the different effect that Christ's miracles had to convince the disciples from what they had to convince the Scribes and Pharisees. Not that they had a stronger reason, or had their reason more improved; but their reason was sanctified, and those blinding prejudices, that the Scribes and Pharisees were under, were removed by the sense they had of the excellency of Christ and his doctrine.

- *[Also indirectly,] it not only removes the hindrances of reason, but positively helps rcason.* It makes even the speculative notions the more lively. It engages the attention of the mind, with the fixedness and intenseness to that kind of objects; which causes it to have a clearer view of them, and enables it more clearly to see their mutual relations, and occasions it to take more notice of them. The ideas themselves that otherwise are dim and obscure, are by this means impressed with the greater strength, and have a light cast upon them; so that the mind can better judge of them. As he that beholds the objects on the face of the earth, when the light of the sun is cast upon them; so that the mind can better judge of them. As he that beholds the objects on the face of the earth, when the light of the sun is cast upon them, is under greater advantage to discern them in their true forms and mutual relations, than he that sees them in a dim starlight or twilight.

The mind having a sensibleness of the excellency of divine objects, dwells upon them with delight; and the powers of the soul are more awakened and enlivened to employ themselves in the contemplation of them, and exert themselves more fully and much more to the purpose. The beauty and sweetness of the objects draws on the faculties, and draws forth their exercises: so that reason itself is under far greater advantages for its proper and free exercises, and to attain its proper end, free of darkness and delusion.

But, *[also, directly:]*

- *A true sense of the divine excellency of the things of God's word doth more directly and immediately convince of the truth of them; and that because the excellency of these things is so superlative.* There is a beauty in them that is so divine and godlike, that is greatly and evidently distinguishing of them from things merely human, or that men are the inventors and authors of; a glory that is so high and great, that when clearly seen, commands assent to their divinity and reality. When there is an actual and lively discovery of this beauty and excellency, it will not allow of any such thought as that it is a human work, or the fruit of men's invention. This evidence that they that are spiritually enlightened have of the truth of the things of religion, is a kind of intuitive and immediate evidence. They believe the doctrines of God's word to be divine, because they see divinity in them; i.e., they see a divine, and transcendent, and most evidently distinguishing glory in them; such a glory as, if clearly seen, does not leave room to doubt of their being of God, and not of men.

  Such a conviction of the truth of religion as this, arising, these ways, from a sense of the divine excellency of them, is that true spiritual conviction that there is in saving faith. And this original of it, is that by which it is most essentially distinguished from that common assent, which unregenerate men are capable of.

II. I proceed now to the *second* thing proposed, viz., to show how this light is immediately given by God, and not obtained by natural means. And here,

1. *It is not intended that the natural faculties are not made use of in it.* The natural faculties are the subject of this light: and they are the subject in such a manner, that they are not merely passive, but active in it; the acts and exercises of man's understanding are concerned and made use of in it. God, in

letting in this light into the soul, deals with man according to his nature, or as a rational creature; and makes use of his human faculties. But yet this light is not the less immediately from God for that; though the faculties are made use of, it is as the subject and not as the cause; and that acting of the faculties in it, is not the cause, but is either implied in the thing itself (in the light that is imparted) or is the consequence of it. As the use that we make of our eyes in beholding various objects, when the sun arises, is not the cause of the light that discovers those objects to us.

2. It is not intended that outward means have no concern in this affair. As I have observed already, it is not in this affair, as it is in inspiration, where new truths are suggested: for here is by this light only given a due apprehension of the same truths that are revealed in the word of God; and therefore it is not given without the word. The gospel is made use of in this affair: this light is the "light of the glorious gospel of Christ," 2 Cor. 4:4. The gospel is as a glass by which this light is conveyed to us, 1 Cor. 13:12. "Now we see through a glass."

3. But, when it is said that this light is given immediately by God, and not obtained by natural means, hereby is intended, that it is given by God without making use of any means that operate by their own power, or a natural force God makes use of means; but it is not as mediate causes to produce this effect. There are not truly any second causes of it; but it is produced by God immediately. The word of God is no proper cause of this effect: it does not operate by any natural force in it. The word of God is only made use of to convey to the mind the subject matter of this saving instruction: and this indeed it doth convey to us by natural force or influence. It conveys to our minds these and those doctrines; it is the cause of the notion of them in our heads, but not of the sense of the divine excellency of them in our hearts. Indeed a person cannot have spiritual light without the word. But that does not argue, that the word properly causes that light. The mind cannot see the excellency of any doctrine, unless that doctrine be first in the mind; but the seeing of the excellency of the doctrine may be immediately from the Spirit of God; though the conveying of the doctrine or proposition itself may be by the word. So that the notions that are the subject matter of this light, are conveyed to the mind by the word of God; but that due sense of the heart, wherein this light formally consists, is immediately by the Spirit of God. As for instance, that notion that there is a Christ, and that Christ is holy and gracious, is conveyed to the mind by the word of God: but the sense of the excellency of Christ by reason of that holiness and grace, is nevertheless immediately the work of the Holy Spirit.

III. I come now, to show the truth of the doctrine; that is, to show that there is such a thing as that spiritual light that has been described, thus immediately let into the mind by God. And here I would show briefly, that this doctrine is both *scriptural* and *rational.*

1. *It is scriptural.* My text is not only full to the purpose, but it is a doctrine that the Scripture abounds in. We are there abundantly taught, that the saints differ from the ungodly in this, that they have the knowledge of God, and a sight of God, and of Jesus Christ. I shall mention but few texts of many. 1 John 3:6, "Whosoever sinneth, has not seen him, nor known him." 3 John 11, "He that doth good, is of God: but he that doth evil, hath not seen God." John 14:19, "The world seeth me no more; but ye see me." John 17:3, "And this is eternal life, that they might know thee, the only true God, and Jesus Christ whom thou hast sent." This knowledge, or sight of God and Christ, cannot be a mere speculative knowledge; because it is spoken of as a seeing and knowing, wherein they differ from the ungodly. And by these Scriptures it must not only be a different knowledge in degree and circumstances, and different in its effects; but it must be entirely different in nature and kind.

And this light and knowledge is always spoken of as immediately given of God, Matt. 11:25–27:

> At that time Jesus answered and said, "I thank thee O Father, Lord of heaven and earth, because thou hast hid these things from the wise and prudent, and hast revealed them unto babes. Even so, Father, for so it seemed good in thy sight. All things are delivered unto me of my Father: and no man knoweth the Son but the Father: neither knoweth any man the Father, save the Son, and he to whomsoever the Son will reveal him."

Here this effect is ascribed alone to the arbitrary operation, and gift of God, bestowing this knowledge on whom he will, and distinguishing those with it, that have the least natural advantage or means for knowledge, even babes, when it is denied to the wise and prudent. And the imparting of the knowledge of God is here appropriated to the Son of God, as his sole prerogative. And again, 2 Cor. 4:6,

> For God, who commanded the light to shine out of darkness, hath shined in our hearts, to give the light of the knowledge of the glory of God, in the face of Jesus Christ.

This plainly shows, that there is such a thing as a discovery of the divine superlative glory and excellency of God and Christ, and that peculiar to the saints: and also, that it is as immediately from God, as light from the sun: and that it is the immediate effect of his power and will; for it is compared to God's creating the light by his powerful word in the beginning of the creation; and is said to be by the Spirit of the Lord, in the 18th verse of the preceding chapter. God is spoken of as giving the knowledge of Christ in conversion, as of what before was hidden and unseen in that. Gal. 1:15,16, "But when it pleased God, who separated me from my mother's womb, and called me by his grace, to reveal his Son in me."

The Scripture also speaks plainly of such a knowledge of the word of God, as has been described, as the immediate gift of God, Psalm 119:18: "Open thou mine eyes, that I may behold wondrous things out of thy law." What could the Psalmist mean when he begged of God to open his eyes? Was he ever blind? Might he not have resort to the law and see every word and sentence in it when he pleased? And what could he mean by those wondrous things? Was it the wonderful stories of the creation, and deluge, and Israel's passing through the Red Sea, and the like? Were not his eyes open to read these strange things when he would? Doubtless by wondrous things in God's law, he had respect to those distinguishing and wonderful excellencies, and marvelous manifestations of the divine perfections, and glory, that there was in the commands and doctrines of the word, and those works and counsels of God that were there revealed. So the Scripture speaks of a knowledge of God's dispensation, and covenant of mercy, and way of grace towards his people, as peculiar to the saints, and given only by God, Psalm 25:14: "The secret of the Lord is with them that fear him; and he will show them his covenant."

And that a true and saving belief of the truth of religion is that which arises from such a discovery, is also what the Scripture teaches. As John 6:40, "And this is the will of him that sent me, that every one which seeth the Son, and believeth on him, may have everlasting life;" where it is plain that a true faith is what arises from a spiritual sight of Christ, and John 17:6–8,

> I have manifested thy name unto the men which thou gavest me out of the world. Now they have known that all things whatsoever thou hast given me, are of thee. For I have given unto them the words which thou gavest me; and they have received them, and have known surely that I came out from thee, and they have believed that thou didst send me;

where Christ's manifesting God's name to the disciples, or giving them the knowledge of God, was that whereby they knew that Christ's doctrine was of God, and that Christ himself was of him, proceeded from him, and was sent by him. Again, John 12:44–46:

> Jesus cried and said, "He that believeth on me, believeth not on me, but on him that sent me. And he that seeth me, seeth him that sent me. I am come a light into the world, that whosoever believeth on me, should not abide in darkness."

Their believing in Christ, and spiritually seeing him, are spoken of as running parallel.

Christ condemns the Jews that they did not know that he was the Messiah, and that his doctrine was true, from an inward distinguishing taste and relish of what was divine, in Luke 12:56,57. He having there blamed the Jews, that though they could discern the face of the sky and of the earth, and signs of the weather, that yet they could not discern those times; or as it is expressed in Matthew, the signs of those times; he adds, yea, and why even of your own selves, judge ye not what is right? i.e., without extrinsic signs. Why have ye not that sense of true excellency, whereby ye may distinguish that which is holy and divine? Why have ye not that savor of the things of God, by which you may see the distinguishing glory, and evident divinity of me and my doctrine?

The Apostle Peter mentions it as what gave them (the apostles) good and well grounded assurance of the truth of the gospel, that they had seen the divine glory of Christ. 2 Pet. 1:16,

> For we have not followed cunningly devised fables when we made known unto you the power and coming of our Lord Jesus Christ, but were eyewitnesses of his majesty.

The apostle has respect to that visible glory of Christ which they saw in his transfiguration: that glory was so divine, having such an ineffable appearance and semblance of divine holiness, majesty and grace, that it evidently denoted him to be a divine person. But if a sight of Christ's outward glory might give a rational assurance of his divinity, why may not an apprehension of his spiritual glory do so too? Doubtless Christ's spiritual glory is in itself as distinguishing, and as plainly showing his divinity, as his outward glory, and a great deal more: for his spiritual glory is that wherein his divinity consists; and the outward glory of his transfiguration showed him to be divine, only as it was a remarkable image or representation of that spiritual glory. Doubtless, therefore, he that has had a clear sight of the spiritual glory of Christ, may say, "I have not followed cunningly devised fables, but have been an eyewitness of his majesty," upon as good grounds as the apostle, when he had respect to the outward glory of Christ that he had seen. But this brings me to what was proposed next, viz., to show that:

2. *This doctrine is rational.*

First, it is rational to suppose, that there is really such an excellency in divine things, that is so transcendent and exceedingly different from what is in other things, that, if it were seen, would most evidently distinguish them. We cannot rationally doubt but that things that are divine, that appertain to the Supreme Being, are vastly different from things that are human; that there is that godlike, high and glorious excellency in them, that does most remarkably difference them from the things that are of men; insomuch that if the difference were but seen, it would have a convincing, satisfying influence upon anyone, that they are what they are, viz., divine. What reason can be offered against it? Unless we would argue, that God is not remarkably distinguished in glory from men.

If Christ should now appear to anyone as he did on the mount at his transfiguration; or if he should appear to the world in the glory that he now appears in, as he will do at the day of judgment; without doubt, the glory and majesty that he would appear in, would be such as would satisfy every one that he was a divine person, and that religion was true: and it would be a most reasonable, and well grounded conviction too. And why may there not be that stamp of divinity, or divine glory on the word of God, on the scheme and doctrine of the gospel, that may be in like manner distinguishing and as rationally convincing, provided it be but seen? It is rational to suppose, that when God speaks to the world, there should be something in his word or speech vastly different from man's word. Supposing that God never had spoken to the world, but we had noticed that he was about to do it; that he was about to reveal himself from heaven, and speak to us immediately himself, in divine speeches or discourses, as it were from his own mouth, or that he should give us a book of his own inditing [writing, dictation]; after what manner should we expect that he would speak? Would it not be rational to suppose, that his speech would be exceeding different from man's speech, that he should speak like a God; that is, that there should be such an excellency and sublimity in his speech or word, such a stamp of wisdom, holiness, majesty and other divine perfections, that the word of man, yea of the wisest of men, should appear mean and base in comparison of it? Doubtless it would be thought rational to expect this, and unreasonable to think otherwise. When a wise man speaks in the exercise of his wisdom, there is something in every thing he says, that is very distinguishable from the talk of a little child. So, without doubt, and much more, is the speech of God (if there be any such thing as the speech of God) to be distinguished from that of the wisest of men; agreeably to Jer. 23:28,29. God having there been reproving the false prophets that prophesied in his name, and pretended that what they spake was his word, when indeed it was their own word, says,

> "The prophet that hath a dream, let him tell a dream; and he that hath my word, let him speak my word faithfully: what is the chaff to the wheat?" saith the Lord. "Is not my word like as a fire?" saith the Lord; "and like a hammer that breaketh the rock in pieces?"

Secondly, if there be such a distinguishing excellency in divine things; it is rational to suppose that there may be such a thing as seeing it. What should hinder but that it may be seen? It is no argument, that there is no such thing as such a distinguishing excellency, or that, if there be, that it cannot be seen, that some do not see it, though they may be discerning men in temporal matters. It is not rational to suppose, if there be any such excellency in divine things, that wicked men should see it. It is not rational to suppose, that those whose minds are full of spiritual pollution, and under the power of filthy lusts, should have any relish or sense of divine beauty or excellency; or that their minds should be susceptive of that light that is in its own nature so pure and heavenly. It need not seem at all strange, that sin should so blind the mind, seeing that men's particular natural tempers and dispositions will so much blind them in secular matters; as when men's natural temper is melancholy, jealous, fearful, proud, or the like.

Third, it is rational to suppose, that this knowledge should be given immediately by God, and not be obtained by natural means. Upon what account should it seem unreasonable, that there should be any immediate communication between God and the creature? It is strange that men should make any matter of difficulty of it. Why should not he that made all things, still have something immediately to do with the things that he has made? Where lies the great difficulty, if we own the being of a God, and that he created all things out of nothing, of allowing some immediate influence of God on the creation still? And if it be reasonable to suppose it with respect to any part of the creation, it is especially so with respect to reasonable, intelligent creatures; who are next to God in the gradation of the different orders of beings, and whose business is most immediately with God; who were made on purpose for those exercises that do respect God and wherein they have nextly to do with God: for reason teaches, that man was made to serve and glorify his Creator. And if it be rational to suppose that God immediately communicates himself to man in any affair, it is in this. It is rational to suppose that God would reserve that knowledge and wisdom, that is of such a divine and excellent nature, to be bestowed immediately by himself, and that it should not be left in the power of second causes. Spiritual wisdom and grace is that highest and most excellent gift that ever God bestows on any creature: in this the highest excellency and perfection of a rational creature consists. It is also immensely the most important of all divine gifts: it is that wherein man's happiness consists, and on which his everlasting welfare depends. How rational is it to suppose that God, however he has left meaner goods and lower gifts to second causes, and in some sort in their power, yet should reserve this most excellent, divine, and important of all divine communications, in his own hands, to be bestowed immediately by himself, as a thing too great for second causes to be concerned in!

It is rational to suppose, that this blessing should be immediately from God; for there is no gift or benefit that is in itself so nearly related to the divine nature, there is nothing the creature receives that is so much of God, of his nature, so much a participation of the deity: it is a kind of emanation of God's beauty, and is related to God as the light is to the sun. It is therefore congruous and fit, that when it is given of God, it should be nextly from himself, and by himself, according to his own sovereign will.

It is rational to suppose, that it should be beyond a man's power to obtain this knowledge and light by the mere strength of natural reason; for it is not a thing that belongs to reason, to see the beauty and loveliness of spiritual things; it is not a speculative thing, but depends on the sense of the heart. Reason indeed is necessary in order to it, as it is by reason only that we are become the subjects of the means of it; which means I have already shown to be necessary in order to it, though they have no proper causal in the affair. It is by reason that we become possessed of a notion of those doctrines that are the subject matter of this divine light; and reason may many ways be indirectly and remotely an advantage to it. And reason has also to do in the acts that are immediately consequent on this discovery: a seeing the truth of religion from hence, is by reason; though it be but by one step, and the inference be immediate. So reason has to do in that accepting of, and trusting in Christ, *that* is consequent on it. But if we take *reason* strictly—not for the faculty of mental perception in general, but for ratiocination, or a power of inferring by arguments—the perceiving of spiritual beauty and excellency no more belongs to reason, than it belongs to the sense of feeling to perceive colors, or to the power of seeing to perceive the sweetness of food. It is out of reason's province to perceive the beauty or loveliness of anything: such a perception does not belong to that faculty. Reason's work is to perceive truth and not excellency. It is not ratiocination that gives men the perception of the beauty and amiableness of a countenance, though it may be many ways indirectly an advantage to it; yet it is no more reason that immediately perceives it, than it is reason that perceives the sweetness of honey: it depends on the sense of the heart. Reason may determine that a countenance is beautiful to others; it may determine that honey is sweet to others; but it will never give me a perception of its sweetness.

IV. I will conclude with a very brief improvement of what has been said.

1. *This doctrine may lead us to reflect on the goodness of God, that has so ordered it, that a saving evidence of the truth of the gospel is such, as is attainable by persons of mean capacities and advantages, as well as those that are of the greatest parts and learning.* If the evidence of the gospel depended only on history, and such reasonings as learned men only are capable of, it would be above the reach of far the greatest part of mankind. But persons with but an ordinary degree of knowledge, are capable, without a long and subtle train of reasoning, to see the divine excellency of the things of religion: they are capable of being taught by the Spirit of God, as well as learned men. The evidence that is this way obtained, is vastly better and more satisfying, than all that can be obtained by the arguings of those that are most learned, and greatest masters of reason. And babes are as capable of knowing these things, as the wise and prudent; and they are often hid from these things, as the wise and prudent; and they are often hid from these when they are revealed to those. 1 Cor. 1:26,27:

> For ye see your calling, brethren, how that not many wise men, after the flesh, not many mighty, not many noble are called. But God hath chosen the foolish things of the world.

2. *This doctrine may well put us upon examining ourselves, whether we have ever had this divine light, that has been described, let into our souls.* If there be such a thing indeed, and it be not only a notion or whimsy of persons of weak and distempered brains, then doubtless it is a thing of great importance, whether we have thus been taught by the Spirit of God; whether the light of the glorious gospel of Christ, who is the image of

God, hath shined unto us, giving us the light of the knowledge of the glory of God in the face of Jesus Christ; whether we have seen the Son, and believed on him, or have that faith of gospel-doctrines which arises from a spiritual sight of Christ.

3. *All may hence be exhorted earnestly to seek this spiritual light.* To influence and move to it, the following things may be considered.

First, this is the most excellent and divine wisdom that any creature is capable of. It is more excellent than any human learning; it is far more excellent than all the knowledge of the greatest philosophers or statesmen. Yea, the least glimpse of the glory of God in the face of Christ doth more exalt and ennoble the soul, than all the knowledge of those that have the greatest speculative understanding in divinity without grace. This knowledge has the most noble object that is or can be, viz., the divine glory or excellency of God and Christ. The knowledge of these objects is that wherein consists the most excellent knowledge of the angels, yea, of God himself.

Secondly, this knowledge is that which is above all others sweet and joyful. Men have a great deal of pleasure in human knowledge, in studies of natural things; but this is nothing to that joy which arises from this divine light shining into the soul. This light gives a view of those things that are immensely the most exquisitely beautiful, and capable of delighting the eye of the understanding. This spiritual light is the dawning of the light of glory in the heart. There is nothing so powerful as this to support persons in affliction, and to give the mind peace and brightness in this stormy and dark world.

Third, this light is such as effectually influences the inclination, and changes the nature of the soul. It assimilates our nature to the divine nature, and changes the soul into an image of the same glory that is beheld. 2 Cor. 3:18,

> But we all with open face, beholding as in a glass the glory of the Lord, are changed into the same image, from glory to glory, even as by the Spirit of the Lord.

This knowledge will wean from the world, and raise the inclination to heavenly things. It will turn the heart to God as the fountain of good, and to choose him for the only portion. This light, and this only, will bring the soul to a saving close[ness] with Christ. It conforms the heart to the gospel, [and] mortifies its enmity and opposition against the scheme of salvation therein revealed: it causes the heart to embrace the joyful tidings, and entirely to adhere to, and acquiesce in the revelation of Christ as our Savior: it causes the whole soul to accord and symphonize with it, admitting it with entire credit and respect, cleaving to it with full inclination and affection; and it effectually disposes the soul to give up itself entirely to Christ.

Fourth, this light, and this only, has its fruit in a universal holiness of life. No merely notional or speculative understanding of the doctrines of religion will ever bring to this. But this light, as it reaches the bottom of the heart, and changes the nature, so it will effectually dispose to a universal obedience. It shows God's worthiness to be obeyed and served. It draws forth the heart in a sincere love to God, which is the only principle of a true, gracious, and universal obedience; and it convinces of the reality of those glorious rewards that God has promised to them that obey him.

Praise, One of the Chief Employments of Heaven

Thanksgiving Sermon, Nov. 7, 1734.

"And I heard a voice from heaven, as the voice of many waters, and as the voice of a great thunder; and I heard the voice of harpers harping with their harps."—Revelation 14:2

We may observe in these words:

- What it was that John heard, viz. the voice and melody of a company praising God. It is said in the next verse that they sung a new song before the throne.
- Whence he heard this voice, "I heard," says he, "a voice from heaven." This company that he heard praising God was in heaven. It is said in the following verse, "They sung this song before the throne, and before the four living creatures, and the elders." But the throne of God, and the four living creatures, and the four and twenty elders, are all represented in these visions of John, as being in heaven. So that this voice was the voice of the heavenly inhabitants,

the voice of the blessed and glorious company that is in heaven, before the throne of God there.

- The kind of voice, which is here set forth in a very lively and elegant manner. It is said to be as the voice of many waters, and as the voice of mighty thunders, and as the voice of harpers harping with their harps.

  Hereby several things are represented in a very striking manner.

  - *The distance of the voice.*
  - *That it was the voice of a vast and innumerable multitude, so that it was as the voice of many waters.* How naturally does this represent the joint, continual, and loud voice of a vast multitude at a distance, that it resembled the voice of many waters?
  - *The loudness of the voice.* It was as the voice of many waters, and as the voice of a great thunder; which describes the extraordinary fervency of their praises, and how lively and vigorous they were therein, and how that everyone praised God with all his might. They all, joining together, sang with such fervency, that heaven did, as it were, ring with their praises. The noise of thunder, and the roaring of many waters, are the most great and majestic sounds ever heard upon earth, and are often spoken of in the Scriptures as the mightiest sounds. John could not distinctly hear what they sang, but they being in heaven, at a great distance, he knew not what better to compare it to, than to the roaring of the sea, or a great thunder.
  - *Yet, it was a melodious sound,* signified by this expression, "I heard the voice of harpers harping with their harps." The harp was a stringed instrument that David made much use of in praising God. John represents the matter thus to us, that the voice which he heard, being at a great distance, it was in distinct; and being of such a vast multitude, and such a mighty fervent voice, that it seemed in some measure like distant thunder, or the roaring of water, and yet he could perceive the music of the voice at the same time. Though it was in some respects as thunder and the noise of water, yet there was a sweet and excellent melody in it.

In short, these comparisons of which John makes use, to signify to us what kind of a voice and sound it was that he heard, are exceedingly lively and elegant. Yet this seems to be evident from them, that what he heard was inexpressible, and that he could find nothing that could perfectly represent it. That a voice should be as the voice of many waters, and as the voice of a great thunder, and yet like the voice of harpers, is to us not easily to be conceived of. But the case was, that John could find no earthly sound that was sufficient to represent it; and therefore such various and different similitudes are aggregated and cast together to represent it. But thus much seems to be signified by it, that it seemed to be the voice of an innumerable multitude, and that they were exceedingly fervent and mighty in their praises. That the voice of this multitude was very great, and exceedingly full of majesty, and yet a most sweet and melodious voice at the same time.

Doctrine

The work of the saints in heaven doth very much consist in praising God.

I. Proposition. The saints in heaven are employed.

They are not idle. They have there much to do. They have a work before them that will fill up eternity.

We are not to suppose, when the saints have finished their course and done the works appointed them here in this world, and are got to their journey's end, to their Father's house, that they will have nothing to do. It is true, the saints when they get to heaven, rest from their labors and their works follow them. Heaven is not a place of labor and travail, but a place of rest. (Heb. 4:9.) There remaineth a rest for the people of God. And it is a place of the reward of labor. But yet the rest of heaven does not consist in idleness, and a cessation of all action, but only a cessation from all the trouble and toil and tediousness of action. The most perfect rest is consistent with being continually employed.

So it is in heaven. Though the saints are exceedingly full of action, yet their activity is perfectly free from all labor, or weariness, or unpleasantness. They shall rest from their work, that is, from all work of labor and self-denial, and grief, care, and watchfulness, but they will not cease from action. The saints in glory are represented as employed in serving God, as well as the saints on earth, though it be without any difficulty or opposition. Rev. 22:3, "And there shall be no more curse: but the throne of God and of the Lamb shall be in it; and his servants shall serve him." Yea, we are told, that they shall serve God day and night, that is, continually or without ceasing. Rev. 7:15, "Therefore are they before the throne of God, and serve him day and night in his temple." And yet this shall be without any manner of trouble, as it follows in the next verse. "They shall hunger no more, neither thirst any more, neither shall the sun light on them nor any heat." In this world, saints labor, as it were, in the wearisome heat of the sun. But there, though they shall still serve God, yet shall the sun not light on them nor any heat. In one sense, the saints and angels in heaven rest not day nor night, Rev. 4:8, that is, they never cease from their blessed employment.

Perfection of happiness does not consist in idleness, but on the contrary, it very much consists in action. The angels are blessed spirits, and yet they are exceedingly active in serving God. They are as a flame of fire, which is the most active thing that we see in this world. God himself enjoys infinite happiness and prefect bliss, and yet he is not inactive, but is himself in his own nature a perfect act, and is continually at work in bringing to pass his own purposes and ends. That principle of holiness that is in its perfection in the saints in heaven, is a most active principle. So that though they enjoy perfect rest, yet they are a great deal more active than they were when in this world. In this world they were exceedingly dull, and heavy, and inactive, but now they are a flame of fire. The saints in heaven are not merely passive in their happiness. They do not merely enjoy God passively, but in an active manner. They are not only acted upon by God, but they mutually act towards him, and in this action and re-action consists the heavenly happiness.

II. Proposition. Their employment consists very much in praising God.

John the beloved disciple had often visions of heaven, and in almost every instance had a vision of the inhabitants as praising God. So in the fourth chapter he tells us, that he looked, and behold, a door was opened in heaven, and he was called up thither, and that he saw the throne of God and him that sat on the throne. And there he gives us an account how those that were round about the throne were praising God. The four living creatures rest not day nor night, saying, "Holy, holy, holy, Lord God Almighty, which was, and is, and is to come." And when those living creatures give glory and honor and thanks to him, the four and twenty elders fall down before him and worship him, etc., etc. Again in the fifth chapter, we have an account how they sing praises to Christ, Rev. 5:8, 9, etc. And so in Rev. 7:9, 10, 11, 12. And in Rev. 11:16, 17. And in the twelfth chapter, 10th verse. And in Rev. 15:2, 3, 4. And in the beginning of the nineteenth chapter we have an account how the hosts of heaven sing hallelujahs to God. By all which it most evidently appears, that their work very much consists in praising God and Christ. We have but a very imperfect knowledge of the future state of blessedness, and of their employment. Without doubt they have various employments there. We cannot reasonably question but they are employed in contributing to each other's delight. They shall dwell together in society. They shall also probably be employed in contemplating on God, his glorious perfections, and glorious works, and so gaining knowledge in these things. And doubtless they will be employed many ways that we know nothing of: but this we may determine, that much of their employment consists in praising God, and that for the following reasons.

1. *Because they there see God.* This is a blessedness promised to the saints, that they shall see God, Mat. 5:8. That they see God, sufficiently shows the reason why they praise him. They that see God cannot but praise him. He is a Being of such glory and excellency that the sight of this excellency of his will necessarily influence them that behold it to praise him. Such a glorious sight will awaken and rouse all the powers of the soul, and will irresistibly impel them, and draw them into acts of praise. Such a sight enlarges their souls, and fills them with admiration, and with an unspeakable exultation of spirit.

'Tis from the little that the saints have seen of God, and know of him in this world, that they are excited to praise him in the degree they do here. But here they see but as in a glass darkly; they have only now and then a little glimpse of God's excellency. But then they shall have the transcendent glory and divine excellency of God set in their immediate and full view. They shall dwell in his immediate glorious presence and shall see face to face, 1 Cor. 13:12. *Now* the saints see the glory of God but by a reflected light, as we in the night see the light of the sun reflected from the moon. But in heaven they shall directly behold the Sun of righteousness, and shall look full upon him when shining in all his glory. This being the case, it can be no otherwise, but that they should very much employ themselves in praising God. When they behold the glorious power of God, they cannot but praise that power. When they see God's wisdom that is so wonderful, and infinitely beyond all created wisdom, they cannot but continually praise that wisdom. When they view the infinitely pure and lovely holiness of God, whereby the heavens themselves are not pure in comparison with him, how can they avoid with an exalted heart to praise that beauty of the divine nature! When they see the infinite grace of God, and see what a boundless ocean of mercy and love he is, how can they but celebrate that grace with the highest praise!

2. *They will have another sense of the greatness of the fruits of God's mercy than we have here in this world.* They will not only have a sight of the

glorious attributes of God's goodness and mercy in their beatific vision of God, but they will be sensible of the exceeding greatness of the fruits of it; the greatness of the benefits that he has bestowed. They will have another sense of the greatness and manifoldness of the communications of his goodness to his creation in general. They will be more sensible how that God is the fountain of all good, the Father of lights, from whom proceeds every good and perfect gift. We do now but little consider, in comparison with what we should do, how full the world is of God's goodness, and how it appears in the sun, moon, and stars, and in the earth and seas, with all their fullness, and wheresoever we turn our eyes, and how all ranks and orders of being, from the highest angel to the lowest insect, are dependent upon, and maintained by, the goodness of God. These the saints in heaven clearly see. They see how the universe is replenished with his goodness, and how the communications of his goodness are incessantly issuing from God as from an everflowing fountain, and are poured forth all around in vast profusion into every part of heaven and earth, as light is every moment diffused from the sun.

We have but faint imperfect notions of these things, but the saints in heaven see them with perfect clearness. They have another sense of the greatness of God's goodness to mankind, and to the church, and to them in particular, than any of us have. They have another sense of the greatness of God's goodness in the temporal mercies which God bestowed upon them while they were here in this world, though they know that spiritual mercies are infinitely greater. But especially they have an immensely greater sense of the exceeding greatness of the fruits of God's grace and mercy bestowed in redemption. They have another sense how great a gift the gift of God's only-begotten Son is. They have another sense of the greatness and dignity of the person of Christ, and how great a thing it was for him to become man, and how great a thing it was for him to lay down his life, and to endure the shameful and accursed death of the cross. They have another sense how great the benefits are that Christ has purchased for men, how great a mercy it is to have sin pardoned, and to be delivered from the misery of Hell. They have another sense how dreadful that misery is, for the damned are tormented in the presence of the holy angels and saints, and they see the smoke of their torment; and have another sense what eternity is, and so are proportionably more sensible how great a mercy it is to be delivered from that torment. They have another sense how great a fruit of God's grace it is to be the children of God, and to have a right and title to eternal glory.

They are sensible of the greatness of the benefits that Christ has purchased, by their experience. For they are in possession of the blessedness and glory that he has purchased. They taste the sweetness of it. And therefore they are more sensible what cause they have to praise God for these things. The grace and goodness of God in the work of redemption appears so wonderful to them that their thoughts of it do excite them to the most ardent praise. When they take a view of the grace of God and of the love of Christ in redemption, they see that there is cause that they should exert the utmost of their capacities, and spend an eternity in praising God and the Lamb. It is but a very little that we at best can conceive of the greatness of the benefits of redemption, and therefore we are but little affected by it, and our praises for it are low and dull things.

3. Another reason is [that] they will be perfect in humility. In order to a person's being rightly disposed to the work of praise, he must be an humble person. A proud person is for assuming all praise to himself and is not disposed to ascribe it to God. It is humility only that will enable us to say from the heart, "Not unto us, not unto us, O Lord, but unto thy name be the glory." The humble person admires the goodness and grace of God to him. He sees more how wonderful it is that God should take such notice of him, and show such kindness to him, that is so much below his notice.

Now the saints in heaven have this grace of humility perfected in them. They do as much excel the saints on earth in humility as in other graces. Though they are so much above the saints on earth in holiness and in their exalted state, yet they are vastly more humble than the saints on earth be. They are as much lower in humility as they are higher in honor and happiness. And the reason of it is that they know more of God. They see more of his greatness and infinite highness, and therefore are more sensible how wonderful it is that God should take so much notice of them, to have such communion with them, and give them such a full enjoyment of him.

They are far more sensible what unworthy creatures they have been, that God should bestow such mercies upon them, than the saints on earth. They have a greater sight of the evil of sin. They see more what filthy vile creatures they were by nature, and how dreadfully they provoked God by actual sin, and how they have deserved God's hatred and wrath. The saints in heaven have as much greater a sense of their unworthiness in their natural state than the saints on earth as they have a greater sense of God's glorious excellency. For it is the sight of God's excellency which gives them a sight of their own unworthiness. And therefore they do proportionally admire the love of God to them in giving Christ to die for them, and the love of Christ in being willing to offer himself for their sins, and of the wonderful mercy of God in their conversion, and bestowing eternal life upon them. The humble sense the saints have of their own unworthiness, doth greatly engage and enlarge their hearts in praise to him for his infinite mercy and grace.

4. *Their love to God and Christ will be perfect.* Love is a principal ingredient in the grace of thankfulness. There is a counterfeit thankfulness in which there is no love. But there is love in exercise in all sincere thankfulness. And the greater any person's love is, the more will he be disposed to praise. Love will cause him to delight in the work. He that loves God, proportionably seeks the glory of God, and loves to give him glory.

Now the hearts of the saints in heaven are all, as it were, a pure flame of love. Love is the grace that never faileth. Whether there be prophecies, they shall fail, whether there be knowledge, it shall vanish away. Faith shall cease in vision, and hope in fruition, but love never faileth. The grace of love will be exalted to its greatest height and highest perfection in heaven. And love will vent itself in praise. Heaven will ring with praise because it is full of love to God. This is the reason that great assembly, that innumerable host, [praises] God with such ardency, that their praise is as the voice of many waters, and as the mighty thunderings, because they are animated by so ardent, vigorous, and powerful a principle of divine love.

Application

I. This subject may be applied in the way of *instruction*.

1. *Hence we may learn the excellency of this work of praising God.* That it is a most excellent employment, appears because it is a heavenly employment. It is that work wherein the saints and angels are continually employed.

If we sincerely and frequently praise God, we shall therein be like the heavenly inhabitants, and join with them.

That it is the work of heaven shows it to be the most honorable work. No employment can be a greater honor to a man than to praise God. It is the peculiar dignity of the nature of man, and the very thing wherein his nature is exalted above things without reason, and things without life, that he is made capable of actively glorifying his Creator. Other creatures do glorify God. The sun, moon, and stars, and the earth and waters, and all the trees of the field, and grass and herbs, and fishes and insects do glorify God. (Psa. 19:1–6; Job 12:7, 8.) But herein is the peculiar dignity of the nature of man, that he is capable of glorifying him as a cause, by counsel, understandingly and voluntarily, which is a heavenly work.

2. *This doctrine may give us an idea of the glorious and happy state of the saints in heaven.* It shows how joyfully and gloriously they spend their time. Joy is a great ingredient in praise. There is an exultation of spirit in fervent praise. Praise is the most joyful work in the world. And how joyful a society are they that join together, so many thousands and millions of them, with one heart and one soul, to sing a new song before the throne, that fill heaven with their glorious melody! How joyful they are in their work, appears in the text, by their fervency in it, so that their voices resounded as the voice of many waters, and as the voice of a great thunder. What ineffable joy was there in those harpers whom John heard harping with their harps!

This shows how different a state the saints are in, in heaven, from what they are in this world. Here much of the work to which the saints are called, consists in laboring, in fighting, in toilsome traveling in a waste howling wilderness, in mourning and suffering, and in offering up strong crying and tears. But there in heaven, their work continually is to lift up their joyful songs of praise.

This world is a valley of tears, a world filled with sighs and groans. One is groaning under some bodily pain. Another is mourning and lamenting over a dear departed friend. Another is crying out by reason of the arm of the oppressor. But in heaven there is no mixture of such sounds as these. There is nothing to be heard amongst them but the sweet and glorious melody of God's praises. There is a holy cheerfulness to be seen throughout that blessed society. Rev. 21:4, "And God shall wipe away all tears from their eyes, and there shall be no more death, neither sorrow nor crying." They shall never have anything more to do with sighing and crying; but their eternal work henceforward shall be praise.

This should make us long for heaven, where they spend their time so joyfully and gloriously. The saints especially have reason to be earnestly breathing after that happy state, where they may in so joyful a manner praise God.

3. *This may put natural persons upon reflecting on their own state, that they have no part nor lot in this matter.* You are an alien from the commonwealth of Israel. You are not one of the people of God. You do not belong to their society that are to spend their eternity after that joyful manner, which you have now heard. You have no right nor portion in heaven. If you hereafter come and offer yourself to be admitted into this blessed society, in your

present state; if you come and try to be admitted, you will be thrust out. You will be driven away. If you come and knock, and cry to be admitted to the wedding, saying, "Lord, Lord, open unto us," all will be to no purpose! You will hear no other word except "Depart!" You shall be shut out into outer darkness. You shall not be permitted to sing among the children, but shall be driven out, to howl among dogs. Rev. 22:14, 15:

> Blessed are they that do his commandments, that they may have a right to the tree of life, and may enter in through the gates into the city; for without are dogs. . .

You are in danger of spending eternity, not in joyfully singing praises, but in a quite contrary manner; in weeping, in wailing, and gnashing of teeth, and blaspheming God because of your pains and because of your plagues. You shall see others coming from the east and the west, and sitting down with Abraham, and Isaac, and Jacob, in the kingdom of God, taking their places among that blessed, happy society, and joining their voices in their heavenly music. But you see your lot. You shall have other work to do. Isa. 65:14, "Behold, my servants shall sing for joy of heart; but ye shall cry for sorrow of heart, and howl for vexation of spirit."

II. In the way of *exhortation*.

If it be so that praising God is very much the employment of heaven, hence let all be exhorted to the work and duty of praising God. The following considerations will show why we should be stirred up by this doctrine to this work.

1. *Let it be considered that the church on earth is the same society with those saints who are praising God in heaven.* There is not one church of Christ in heaven, and another here upon earth. Though the one be sometimes called the church triumphant, and the other the church militant, yet they are not indeed two churches. By the church triumphant is meant the triumphant part of the church. And by the church militant, the militant part of it, for there is but one universal or catholic church. Song [of Songs] 6:9: "My dove, my undefiled, is but one." Christ has and hath many members. The glorious assembly and the saints on earth make but one family. Eph. 3:15, "Of whom the whole family in heaven and earth is named." Though some are in heaven, and some on earth, in very different circumstances, yet they are all united. For there is but "one body, and one spirit, and one Lord Jesus Christ. One God and Father of all, who is above all, and

through all, and in all." God hath in Christ united the inhabitants of heaven, and the holy inhabitants of this earth, and hath made them one. Eph. 1:10:

> That in the dispensation of the fulness of time, he might gather together in one all things in Christ, both which are in heaven, and which are on earth, even in him.

Heaven is at a great distance from the earth. It is called a "far country," Mat. 25:14. Yet the distance of place does not separate them so as to make two societies. For though the saints on earth, at present, are at a distance from heaven, yet they belong there. That is their proper home. The saints that are in this world are strangers here. And therefore the apostle reproved the Christians in his day, for acting as though they belonged to this world. Col. 2:20, "Why, as though living in the world, are ye subject to ordinances?"

Some of a people may be in their own land, and some in a strange land. And yet be but one people. Some of a family may be at home, and some sojourning abroad. And yet be but one family. The saints on earth, though they be not actually in heaven, yet have their inheritance in heaven, and are traveling towards heaven, and will arrive there in a little time. They are nearly related to the saints in heaven. They are their brethren, being children of the same Father, and fellow heirs with Jesus Christ. In Eph. 2:19, the saints on earth are said to be "fellow citizens with the saints, and of the household of God." And the apostle tells the Christian Hebrews, Heb. 12:22–24, that they were

> come to Mount Zion, and to the city of the living God, the heavenly Jerusalem, and to an innumerable company of angels, to the general assembly and church of the first-born, which are written in heaven, and to God the Judge of all, and to the spirits of just men made perfect.

But how were they *come* to this heavenly city, and this glorious assembly, when they were yet here on earth? They were come to them, ere they were brought and united to them in the same family.

But this is what I would inculcate by all this, that the church of God on earth ought to be employed in the same work with the saints in heaven, because they are the same society. As they are but one family, have but one Father, one inheritance, so they should have but one work. The church on earth ought to join with the saints in heaven in their employment, as God hath joined them in one society by his grace.

We profess to be of the visible people of Christ, to be Christians and not heathens, and so belong to the universal church. We profess therefore to be of the same society, and shall not walk answerably to our profession, unless we employ ourselves in the same work.

2. Let it be considered, that we all of us hope to spend an eternity with the saints in heaven, and in the same work of praising God. There is, it may be, not one of us but who hopes to be a saint in heaven, and there continually to sing praises to God and the Lamb. But how disagreeable will it be with such a hope, to live in the neglect of praising God now! We ought now to begin that work which we intend shall be the work of another world. For this life is given us on purpose that therein we might prepare for a future life.

The present state is a state of probation and preparation, a state of preparation for the enjoyments and employment of another, future, and eternal state. And no one is ever admitted to those enjoyments and employments, but those who are prepared for them here. If ever we would go to heaven, we must be fitted for heaven in this world.

We must here have our souls molded and fashioned for that work and that happiness. They must be formed for praise, and they must begin their work here. The beginnings of future things are in this world. The seed must be sown here. The foundation must be laid in this world. Here is laid the foundation of future misery, and of future happiness. If it be not begun here, it never will be begun. If our hearts be not in some measure tuned to praise in this world, we shall never do anything at the work hereafter.

The light must dawn in this world, or the sun will never rise in the next. As we therefore all of us would be, and hope to be, of that blessed company which praise God in heaven, we should now inure ourselves to the work.

3. Those works of God's mercy for which the saints in heaven will chiefly praise him, have been wrought amongst us in this world.

The mercy and grace of God for which the saints in heaven will chiefly praise him is his mercy exercised in the work of redemption, which work has been wrought out in this world. This love of God is the chief object of their admiration, and what they chiefly contemplate, and that employs their most ardent praises.

The grace of Christ, about which their praises will be principally employed, is that he should so love sinful man as to undertake for him, to take upon him man's nature, and lay down his life for him. We find that is the subject of their praises in Rev. 5:8, 9:

> And when he had taken the book, the four living creatures, and the four and twenty elders, fell down before the Lamb, having every one of them harps, and golden vials full of odors, which are the prayers of saints; and they sang a new song, "Thou art worthy, for thou hast redeemed us to God by thy blood."

They will chiefly praise God for these fruits of his mercy, because these are the greatest fruits of it that ever have been, far greater than the glorifying of saints. The saints in heaven will praise God for bestowing glory upon them. But the actual bestowment of glory upon them, after it has been purchased by the blood of Christ, is in no measure so great a thing as the purchasing of it by his blood. For Christ, the eternal Son of God, to become man, and to lay down his life, was a far greater thing than the glorifying of all the saints that ever have been, or ever will be glorified, from the beginning of the world to the end of it. The giving Christ to die, comprehends all other mercies. For all other mercies are through this. The giving of Christ is a greater thing than the giving of all things else for the sake of Christ. This evidently appears, from Rom. 8:32, "He who spared not his own Son, but delivered him up for us all, how shall he not with him also freely give us all things?" So that the work of redemption is that for which the saints in heaven do chiefly praise God. But this work has been wrought here, among us in this world. "The Word was made flesh, and dwelt among us." The incarnation of Christ was a thing that was brought to pass in this world, and the sufferings and death of Christ were also accomplished on earth. Shall heaven be filled with praises for what was done on earth, and shall there be no praises on earth where it was done?

4. *If you praise God sincerely in this world, it will be a sign that you are really to be one of those that shall praise him in heaven.* If any man be found sincerely glorifying God, he will in due time be brought to them, as one who is fit to be of their company. Heaven is the appointed place of all sincere praisers of God. They are all to be gathered together there. And no man can sincerely praise God unless he be one of those who are redeemed from among men, one that God has separated from the rest of the world, and set apart for himself.

5. *If we begin now to exercise ourselves in the work of heaven, it will be the way to have foretastes of the enjoyments of heaven.* The business and the happiness go together. This will be the way to have your heart filled with

spiritual joy and comfort. If you heartily praise God, you shall rejoice in him, and he will show you more of himself, of his glory and love, that you may still have greater cause of praise.

III. I proceed to give some *directions* for the performance of this work.

1. Be directed, in order to your acceptably performing this duty, to repent of your sins, and turn to God. If you have not a work of conversion wrought in you, you will do nothing to any purpose in this work of praise. An unconverted person never once sincerely or acceptably praises God. If you would do the work of the saints in heaven, you must be, not only in profession, but really, one of their society. For there are none else can do their work. As in the verse following the text:

> And they sung as it were a new song, before the throne, and before the four living creatures, and the elders; and no man could learn that song, but the hundred and forty-four thousand, which were redeemed from the earth.

A hundred and forty-four thousand is a mystical number for the church of God, or the assembly of the saints, or those that are redeemed from the earth. There is no man can learn the song that they sing in heaven, but those of that number. It is beyond the reach of all natural men, let them be persons of ever so great abilities and sagacity. They never can learn that heavenly song, if they be not of that number. For it is only the sanctifying, saving instruction of the Spirit of God, that can teach us that song.

2. Labor after more and more of those principles from whence the praise of the saints in heaven doth arise. You have already heard that the saints in heaven do praise the Lord so fervently because they *see* him. Labor therefore that you, though you have not an immediate vision of God, as they have, may yet have a clear spiritual sight of him, and that you may know more of God, and have frequent discoveries of him made to you.

You have heard that the saints in heaven make praise so much their work, because of the great sense they have of the greatness and wonderfulness of the fruits of the Lord's goodness. Labor therefore to get your minds more deeply impressed with such a sense.

The saints in glory are so much employed in praise, because they are perfect in *humility*, and have so great a sense of the infinite distance between God and them. They have a great sense of their own unworthiness, that they are by nature unworthy of any of the mercy of God. Labor therefore that you may obtain more of a sense of your own littleness, and vileness; that you may see more what you are, how ill you have deserved at the hands of God, and how you are less than the least of all his mercies.

The hearts of the saints in heaven are all inflamed with divine *love*, which continually influences them to praise God. Seek that this principle may abound in you, and then you likewise will delight in praising God. It will be a most sweet and pleasant employment to you.

3. Labor, in your praises, to praise God, so far as may be, in the same manner that the saints do in heaven. They praise him *fervently*, with their whole heart, and with all their strength, as was represented in vision to John by the exceeding loudness of their praise. Labor therefore that you may not be cold and dull in your praises, but that you also may praise God fervently.

The saints in heaven praise God *humbly*. Let it also be your delight to abase yourselves, to exalt God, and set him upon the throne, and to lie at his footstool.

The saints in heaven praise God *unitedly*. They praise him with one heart and one soul, in a most firm union. Endeavor that you may thus praise God in union with his people, having your hearts knit to them in fervent love and charity, which will be a great help to your praising and glorifying God unitedly with them.

IV. In the way of *reproof* to those who neglect the *singing* of God's praises.

Certainly, such a neglect is not consonant to the hope and expectation of spending an eternity in that work. It is an appointment of God, that we should not only praise in our prayers, but that we should *sing* his praises. It was a part of divine worship, not only under the Old Testament, but the New. Thus we read that Christ and his disciples sung praises together, Mat. 26:30. So it is commanded, Eph. 5:18, 19:

> Be ye filled with the Spirit, speaking to yourselves in psalms, and hymns, and spiritual songs, singing and making melody in your hearts to the Lord.

And Col. 3:16:

> Let the word of Christ dwell in you richly in all wisdom; teaching and admonishing one another in psalms, and hymns, and spiritual songs, singing with grace in your hearts to the Lord.

1 Cor. 14:15:

> I will sing with the spirit, and I will sing with the understanding also.

So also the saints in heaven are represented as singing God's praises. And is that their happy and glorious employment; and yet shall it be so neglected by us, who hope for heaven?

If there be any of the godly that do neglect this duty, I would desire them to consider how discordant such a neglect is with their profession, with their state, and with the mercies which God has bestowed. How much cause has God given you to sing his praise! You have received more to prompt you to praise God than all the natural men in the world. And can you content yourself to live in the world without singing the praises of your heavenly Father, and your glorious Redeemer?

Parents ought to be careful that their children are instructed in singing, that they may be capable of performing that part of divine worship. This we should do, as we would have our children trained up for heaven, for we all of us would have our children go to heaven.

V. In the way of *consolation* to the godly.

It may be a matter of great comfort to you that you are to spend your eternity with the saints in heaven, where it is so much their work to praise God. The saints are sensible what cause they have to praise God, and oftentimes are ready to say they long to praise him more, and that they never can praise him enough. This may be a consolation to you, that you shall have a whole eternity in which to praise him. They earnestly desire to praise God better. This, therefore, may be your consolation, that in heaven your heart shall be enlarged, you shall be enabled to praise him in an immensely more perfect and exalted manner than you can do in this world. You shall not be troubled with such a dead, dull heart, with so much coldness, so many clogs and burdens from corruption, and from a earthly mind; with a wandering, unsteady heart; with so much darkness and so much hypocrisy. You shall be one of that vast assembly that praise God so fervently, that their voice is "as the voice of many waters, and as the voice of mighty thunderings."

You long to have others praise God, to have everyone praise him. There, there will be enough to help you, and join you in praising him, and those that are capable of doing it ten thousand times better than saints on earth. Thousands and thousands of angels and glorified saints will be around you, all united to you in the dearest love, all disposed to praise God, not only for themselves, but for his mercy to you.

A Farewell Sermon

Edwards was the pastor of the First Church in Northampton, Massachusetts for 23 years, succeeding his grandfather in the position. In this, one of Edwards' rare "personal" sermons, he pours his heart out to the flock he led for over 20 years. "Preached at the first precinct at Northampton after the people's public rejection of their minister, and renouncing their relation to him as pastor of the church there. On June 22, 1750; occasioned by difference of sentiments, concerning the requisite qualifications of members of the church in complete standing." (*Memoirs of Jonathan Edwards*, Vol. 1, p. ccxl.)

Edwards' Preface

It is not unlikely that some of the readers of the following Sermon may be inquisitive concerning the circumstances of the difference between me and the people of Northampton, that issued in that separation between me and them, which occasioned the preaching of this Farewell Sermon.

There is, by no means, room here for a full account of that matter: but yet it seems to be proper, and even necessary, here to correct some gross misrepresentations, which have been abundantly, and (it is to be feared) by some affectedly and industriously made, of that difference. Such as, that I insisted on persons being assured of their being in a state of salvation, in order to my admitting them into the church; that I required a particular relation of the method and order of a person's inward experience, and of the time and manner of his conversion, as the test of his fitness for Christian communion; yea, that I have undertaken to set up a pure church and to make an exact and certain distinction between saints and hypocrites, by a pretended infallible discerning the state of men's souls; that in these things I had fallen in with those wild people, who have lately appeared in New England, called Separatists, and that I myself was become a grand separatist; that I arrogated all the power of judging of the qualifications of candidates for communion wholly to myself, and insisted on acting by my sole authority, in the admission of members into the church, etc.

In opposition to these slanderous representations, I shall at present only give my reader an account of some things which I laid before the council that separated between me and my people, in order to their having a just and full account of my principles, relating to the affair in controversy.

Long before the sitting of the council, my people had sent to the Reverend Mr. Clark of Salem village, desiring him to write in opposition to my principles. Which gave me occasion to write to Mr. Clark, that he might have true information what my principles were. And in the time of the sitting of the council, I did, for their information, make a public declaration of my principles before them and the church, in the meeting-house, of the same import with that in my letter to Mr. Clark, and in very much the same words. And then, afterwards, sent in to the council in writing, an extract of that letter, containing the information I had given Mr. Clark, in the very words of my letter to him, that the council might read and consider it at their leisure, and have a more certain and satisfactory knowledge what my principles were. The extract which I sent in to them was in the following words:

> I am often, and I do not know but pretty generally in the country, represented as of a new and odd opinion with respect to the terms of Christian communion, and as being for introducing a peculiar way of my own.
>
> Whereas, I do not perceive that I differ at all from the scheme of Dr. Watts, in his book entitled, *The Rational Foundation of a Christian Church, and the Terms of Christian communion*; which, he says, is the common sentiment and practice of all reformed churches. I had not seen this book of Dr. Watt's when I published what I have written on the subject. But yet, I think, my sentiments, as I have expressed them, are as exactly agreeable to what he lays down, as if I had been his pupil. Nor do I at all go beyond what Dr. Doddridge plainly shows to be his sentiments, to his *Rise and Progress of Religion*, and his *Sermons on Regeneration*, and his *Paraphrase and Notes on the New Testament*. Nor indeed, Sir, when I consider the senti-

ments you have expressed in your letters to Major Pomroy and Mr. Billing, can I perceive but that they come exactly to the same thing that I maintain.

You suppose [that] the sacraments are not converting ordinances: but that, *as seals of the covenant, they presuppose conversion, especially in the adult; and that it is visible saintship, or, in other words, a credible profession of faith and repentance, a solemn consent to the gospel-covenant, joined with a good conversation, and competent measure of Christian knowledge, is what gives a gospel-right to all sacred ordinances: but that it is necessary to those that come to these ordinances, and in those that profess a consent to the gospel covenant, that they be sincere in their profession,* or at least should think themselves so.

The great thing which I have scrupled in the established method of this church's proceeding, and which I dare no longer go on in, is their publicly assenting to the form of words rehearsed on occasions of their admission to the communion, without pretending thereby to mean any such thing as a hearty consent to the terms of the gospel-covenant, or to mean any such faith or repentance as belong to the covenant of grace, and are the grand conditions of that covenant. It being, at the same time that the words are used, their known and established principle, which they openly profess and proceed upon, that men may and ought to use these words, and mean no such thing, but something else of a nature far inferior; which I think they have no distinct determinate notion of; but something consistent with their knowing that they do not choose God as their chief good, but love the world more than him, and that they do not give themselves up entirely to God but make reserves; and in short, knowing that they do not heartily consent to the gospel-covenant, but live still under the reigning power of the love of the world, and enmity to God and Christ. So that the words of their public profession, according to their openly established use, cease to be of the nature of any profession of gospel faith and repentance, or any proper compliance with the covenant. For it is their profession, that the words, as used, mean no such thing. The words used under these circumstances, do at least fail of being a credible profession of these things.

I can conceive of no such virtue in a certain set of words, that it is proper, merely on the making these sounds, to admit persons to Christian sacraments, without any regard to any pretended meaning of these sounds. Nor can I think, that any institution of Christ has established any such terms of admission into the Christian church.

It does not belong to the controversy between me and my people, how particular or large the profession should be, that is required. I should not choose to be confined to exact limits as to that matter: but rather than contend, I should content myself with a few words, briefly expressing the cardinal virtues or acts implied in a hearty compliance with the covenant, made (as should appear by

> inquiry into the person's doctrinal knowledge) understandingly; if there were an external conversation agreeable thereto. Yea, I should think, that such a person, solemnly making such a profession, had a right to be received as the object of a public charity, however he himself might scruple his own conversion, on account of his not remembering the time, not knowing the method, of his conversion, or finding so much remaining sin, etc. And (if his own scruples did not hinder his coming to the Lord's table) I should think the minister or church had no right to debar such a professor, though he should say he did not think himself converted. For I call that a profession of godliness, which is a profession of the great things wherein godliness consists, and not a profession of his own opinion of his good estate. *(Northampton, May 7, 1750)*

The council, having heard that I had made certain draughts of the covenant, or forms of a public profession of religion which I stood ready to accept of from the candidates for church communion, they, for their further information, sent for them. Accordingly I sent them four distinct draughts or forms, which I had drawn up about a twelvemonth before, as what I stood ready to accept of (any one of them) rather than contend, and break with my people.

The two shortest of these forms are here inserted for the satisfaction of the reader. They are as follows:

> I hope I do truly find a heart to give up myself wholly to God, according to the tenor of that covenant of grace which was sealed in my baptism; and to walk in a way of that obedience to all the commandments of God, which the covenant of grace requires, as long as I live.

Another,

> I hope I truly find in my heart a willingness to comply with all the commandments of God, which require me to give up myself wholly to him, and to serve him with my body and my spirit. And do accordingly now promise to walk in a way of obedience to all the commandments of God, as long as I live.

Such kind of professions as these I stood ready to accept, rather than contend and break with my people. Not but that I think it much more convenient, that ordinarily the public profession of religion that is made by Christians, should be much fuller and more particular. And that (as I hinted in my letter to Mr. Clark) I should not choose to be tied up to any certain form of words, but to have liberty to vary the expressions of a public profession, the more exactly to suit the sentiments and experience of the professor, that it might be a more just and free expression of what each one finds in his heart.

Moreover, it must be noted, that I ever insisted on it, that it [the responsibility] belonged to me as a pastor, before a profession was accepted, to have full liberty to instruct the candidate in the meaning of the terms of it, and in the nature of the things proposed to the professed; and to inquire into his doctrinal understanding of these things, according to my best discretion; and to caution the person, as I should think needful, against rashness in making such a profession, or doing it mainly for the credit of himself or his family, or from any secular views whatsoever, and to put him on serious self-examination, and searching his own heart, and prayer to God to search and enlighten him, that he may not be hypocritical and deceived in the profession he makes; withal pointing forth to him the many ways in which professors are liable to be deceived.

Nor do I think it improper for a minister in such a case, to inquire and know of the candidate what can be remembered of the circumstance of his Christian experience; as this may tend much to illustrate his profession, and give a minister a great advantage for proper instructions: though a particular knowledge and remembrance of the time and method of the first conversion to God, is not be made the test of a person's sincerity, nor insisted on as necessary in order to his being received into full charity. Not that I think it at all improper or unprofitable, that in some special cases, a declaration of the particular circumstances of a person's first awakening, and the manner of his convictions, illuminations, and comforts, should be publicly exhibited before the whole congregation, on occasion of his admission into the church; though this be not demanded as necessary to admission. I ever declared against insisting on a relation of experiences, in this sense (viz. a relation of the particular time and steps of the operation of the Spirit, in first conversion), as the term of communion: yet, if by a relation of experiences, be meant a declaration of experience of the great things wrought, wherein true grace and the essential acts and habits of holiness consist; in this sense, I think an account of a person's experiences [is] necessary in order to his admission into full communion in the church. But that in whatever inquiries are made, and whatever account is given, neither minister nor church are to set up themselves as searchers of hearts, but are to accept the serious solemn profession of the well-instructed professor, of a good life, as best able to determine what he finds in his own heart.

These things may serve in some measure to set right those of my readers who have been misled in their apprehensions of the state of the controversy between me and my people, by the aforementioned misrepresentations.

A Farewell Sermon

"As also you have acknowledged us in part, that we are your rejoicing, even as ye also are ours in the day of the Lord Jesus."—2 Corinthians 1:14

Subject: Ministers and people that are under their care, must meet one another before Christ's tribunal at the day of judgment.

The apostle, in the preceding part of the chapter, declares what great troubles he met with in the course of his ministry. In the text, and two foregoing verses, he declares what were his comforts and supports under the troubles he met with. There are four things in particular.

- That he had approved himself to his own conscience, verse 12: "For our rejoicing is this, the testimony of our conscience, that in simplicity and godly sincerity, not with fleshly wisdom, but by the grace of God, we have had our conversation in the world, and more abundantly to you-wards."
- Another thing he speaks of as matter of comfort, is that as he had approved himself to his own conscience, so he had also to the consciences of his hearers, the Corinthians, to whom he now wrote, and that they should approve of him at the day of judgment.
- The hope he had of seeing the blessed fruit of his labors and sufferings in the ministry, in their happiness and glory, in that great day of accounts.
- That in his ministry among the Corinthians, he had approved himself to his Judge, who would approve and reward his faithfulness in that day.

These three last particulars are signified in my text, and the preceding verse, and indeed all the four are implied in the text. It is implied that the

Corinthians had acknowledged him as their spiritual father, and as one that had been faithful among them, and as the means of their future joy and glory at the day of judgment. It is implied that the apostle expected at that time to have a joyful meeting with them before the Judge, and with joy to behold their glory, as the fruit of his labors, and so they would be his rejoicing. It is implied also that he then expected to be approved of the great Judge, when he and they should meet together before him, and that he would then acknowledge his fidelity, and that this had been the means of their glory, and that thus he would, as it were, give them to him as his crown of rejoicing. But this the apostle could not hope for, unless he had the testimony of his own conscience in his favor. And therefore the words do imply, in the strongest manner, that he had approved himself to his own conscience.

There is one thing implied in each of these particulars, and in every part of the text, which I shall make the subject of my present discourse, viz.

Doctrine

Ministers, and the people that have been under their care, must meet one another before Christ's tribunal at the day of judgment.

Ministers, and the people that have been under their care, must be parted in this world, how well soever they have been united. If they are not separated before, they must be parted by death, and they may be separated while life is continued. We live in a world of change, where nothing is certain or stable, and where a little time, a few revolutions of the sun, brings to pass strange things, surprising alterations, in particular persons in families, in towns and churches, in countries and nations. It often happens, that those who seem most united, in a little time are most disunited, and at the greatest distance. Thus ministers and people, between whom there has been the greatest mutual regard and strictest union, may not only differ in their judgments, and be alienated in affection, but one may rend from the other, and all relation between them be dissolved. The minister may be removed to a distant place, and they may never have any more to do one with another in this world. But if it be so, there is one meeting more that they must have, and that is in the last great day of accounts. Here I would show:

I. In what *manner* ministers, and the people which have been under their care, shall meet one another at the day of judgment.

II. For what *purposes*.

III. For what *reasons* God has so ordered it, that ministers and their people shall then meet together in such a manner, and for such purposes.

I. I would show, in some particulars, in what manner ministers and the people which have been under their care, shall meet one another at the day of judgment.

1. *They shall not meet at the day merely as all the world must then meet together.* I would observe a difference in two things.

First, as to a clear actual view, and distinct knowledge and notice, of each other. Although the whole world will be then present, all mankind of all generations gathered in one vast assembly, with all of the angelic nature, both elect and fallen angels, yet we need not suppose that everyone will have a distinct and particular knowledge of each individual of the whole assembled multitude, which will undoubtedly consist of many millions of millions. Though it is probable that men's capacities will be much greater than in their present state, yet they will not be infinite. Though their understanding and comprehension will be vastly extended, yet men will not be deified. There will probably be a very enlarged view that particular persons will have of the various parts and members of that vast assembly, and so of the proceedings of that great day. But yet it must needs be, that according to the nature of finite minds, some persons and some things, at that day, shall fall more under the notice of particular persons than others. This (as we may well suppose) according as they shall have a nearer concern with some than others in the transactions of the day. There will be special reason why those who have had special concerns together in this world, in their state of probation, and whose mutual affairs will be then to be tried and judged, should especially be set in one another's view. Thus we may suppose, that rulers and subjects, earthly judges and those whom they have judged, neighbors who have had mutual converse, dealings, and contests, heads of families and their children and servants, shall then meet, and in a peculiar distinction be set together. And especially will it be thus with ministers and their people. It is evident by the text, that these shall be in each other's view, shall distinctly know each other, and shall have particular notice one of another at that time.

Secondly, they shall meet together, as having special concern one with another in the great transactions of that day. Although they shall meet the whole world at that time, yet they will not have any immediate and particular concern with all. Yea, the far greater part of those who shall then be gathered together, will be such as they have had no intercourse with in their state of probation, and so will have no mutual concerns to be judged of. But as to ministers and the people that have been under their care, they will be such as have had much immediate concern one with another, in matters of the greatest moment. Therefore they especially must meet, and be brought together before the Judge, as having special concern one with another in the design and business of that great day of accounts. Thus their meeting, as to the manner of it, will be diverse from the meeting of mankind in general.

2. *Their meeting at the day of judgment will be very diverse [different] from their meetings one with another in this world.* Ministers and their people, while their relation continues, often meet together in this world. They are wont to meet from sabbath to sabbath, and at other times, for the public worship of God, and administration of ordinances, and the solemn services of God's house. And besides these meetings, they have also occasions to meet for the determining and managing their ecclesiastical affairs, for the exercise of church discipline, and the settling and adjusting those things which concern the purity and good order of public administrations. But their meeting at the day of judgment will be exceeding diverse, in its manner and circumstances, from any meetings and interviews they have one with another in the present state. I would observe how, in a few particulars.

First: now they meet together in a preparatory mutable state, but then in an unchangeable state. Now *sinners* in the congregation meet their minister in a state wherein they are capable of a saving change, capable of being turned, through God's blessing on the ministrations and labors of their pastor, from the power of Satan unto God; and being brought out of a state of guilt, condemnation, and wrath, to a state of peace and favor with God, to the enjoyment of the privileges of his children, and a title to their eternal inheritance. And *saints* now meet their minister with great remains of corruption, and sometimes under great spiritual difficulties and affliction: and therefore are yet the proper subjects of means for a happy alteration of their state, which they have reason to hope for in the attendance on ordinances, and of which God is pleased commonly to make his ministers the instruments. Ministers and their people now meet in order to the bringing to pass such happy changes: they are the great benefits sought in their solemn meetings.

But when they shall meet together at the day of judgment, it will be far otherwise. They will all meet in an unchangeable state. *Sinners* will be in an unchangeable state. They who then shall be under the guilt and power of sin, and have the wrath of God abiding on them, shall be beyond all remedy or possibility of change, and shall meet their ministers without any hopes of relief or remedy, or getting any good by their means.

And as for the *saints*, they will be already perfectly delivered from all their corruption, temptation, and calamities of every kind, and set forever out of their reach; and no deliverance, no happy alteration, will remain to be accomplished in the use of means of grace, under the administrations of ministers. It will then be pronounced,

> He that is unjust, let him be unjust still; and he that is filthy, let him be filthy still; and he that is righteous, let him be righteous still; and he that is holy, let him be holy still.

Secondly: then they shall meet together in a state of clear, certain, and infallible light. Ministers are set as guides and teachers, and are represented in Scripture as lights set up in the churches, and in the present state meet their people, from time to time, in order to instruct and enlighten them, to correct their mistakes, and to be a voice behind them, when they turn aside to the right hand or the left, saying, "This is the way, walk ye in it;" to evince and confirm the truth by exhibiting the proper evidences of it. They [are] to refute errors and corrupt opinions, to convince the erroneous, and establish the doubting. But when Christ shall come to judgment, every error and false opinion shall be detected. All deceit and delusion shall vanish away before the light of that day, as the darkness of the night vanishes at the appearance of the rising sun. Every doctrine of the Word of God shall then appear in full evidence, and none shall remain unconvinced. All shall know the truth with the greatest certainty, and there shall be no mistakes to rectify.

Now ministers and their people may disagree in their judgments concerning some matters of religion, and may sometimes meet to confer together concerning those things wherein they differ, and to hear the reasons that may be offered on one side and the other; and all may be ineffectual as to any conviction of the truth. They may meet and part again, no more agreed than before, and that side which was in the wrong may remain so still. Sometimes the meetings of ministers with their people, in such a case of disagreeing sentiments, are attended with unhappy debate and controversy, managed with much prejudice and want of candor; not tending to light and conviction, but rather to confirm and increase darkness, and establish opposition to the truth, and alienation of affection one from another. But when they shall meet together at the day of judgment, before the tribunal of the great Judge, the mind and will of Christ will be made known, and there shall no longer be any debate or difference of opinions. The evidence of the truth shall appear beyond all dispute, and all controversies shall be finally and forever decided.

Now ministers meet their people in order to enlighten and awaken the consciences of sinners: setting before them the great evil and danger of sin, the strictness of God's law, their own wickedness of heart and practice, the great guilt they are under, the wrath that abides upon them, and their impotence, blindness, poverty, and helpless and undone condition. But all is often in vain. They remain still, notwithstanding all their ministers can say, stupid and unawakened, and their consciences unconvinced. But it will not be so at their last meeting at the day of judgment. Sinners, when they shall meet their minister before their great Judge, will not meet him with a stupid conscience. They will then be fully convinced of the truth of those things which they formerly heard from him, concerning the greatness and terrible majesty of God, his holiness and hatred of sin, his awful justice in punishing it, the strictness of his law and the dreadfulness and truth of his threatenings, and their own unspeakable guilt and misery. And they shall never more be insensible of these things. The eyes of conscience will now be fully enlightened, and never shall be blinded again. The mouth of conscience shall now be opened, and never shall be shut any more.

Now ministers meet with their people, in public and private, in order to enlighten them concerning the state of their souls; to open and apply the rules of God's Word to them, in order to their searching their own hearts, and discerning their state. But now ministers have no infallible discernment of the state of their people; and the most skillful of them are liable to mistakes, and often are mistaken in things of this nature. Nor are the people able certainly to know the state of their minister, or one another's state: very often those pass among them for saints, and it may be eminent saints, that are grand hypocrites. And on the other hand, those are sometimes censured, or hardly received into their charity, that are indeed some of God's jewels. And nothing is more common than for men to be mistaken concerning their *own* state. Many that are abominable to God, and the children of his wrath, think highly of themselves, as his precious saints and dear children. Yea, there is reason to think that often some that are most bold in their confidence of their safe and happy state, and think themselves not only true saints, but the most eminent saints in the congregation, are in a peculiar manner a smoke in God's nostrils. And thus it undoubtedly often is in those congregations where the Word of God is most faithfully dispensed, notwithstanding all that ministers can say in their clearest explications, and most searching applications of the doctrines and rules of God's Word to the souls of their hearers.

But in the day of judgment they shall have another sort of meeting. Then the secrets of every heart shall be made manifest, and every man's state shall be perfectly known. 1 Cor. 4:5:

> Therefore judge nothing before the time, until the Lord come, who both will bring to light the hidden things of darkness, and will make manifest the counsels of the hearts: and then shall every man have praise of God.

Then none shall be deceived concerning his own state, nor shall be any more in doubt about it. There shall be an eternal end to all the self-conceit and vain hopes of deluded hypocrites, and all the doubts and fears of sincere Christians. And then shall all know the state of one another's souls. The people shall know whether their minister has been sincere and faithful, and the minister shall know the state of every one of their people, and to who the word and ordinances of God have been a savor of life unto life, and to whom a savor of death unto death.

Now in this present state it often happens that when ministers and people meet together to debate and manage their ecclesiastical affairs, especially in a state of controversy, they are ready to judge and censure with regard to each other's views, designs, and the principles and ends by which each is influenced, and are greatly mistaken in their judgment and wrong one another in their censures. But at that future meeting, things will be set in a true and perfect light, and the principles and aims that everyone has acted from, shall be certainly known. There will be an end to all errors of this kind, and all unrighteous censures.

Thirdly: in this world, ministers and their people often meet together to hear of and wait upon an unseen Lord. But at the judgment, they shall meet in his most immediate and visible presence.

Ministers—who now often meet their people to preach to them the King eternal, immortal, and invisible, to convince them that there is a God and declare to them what manner of being he is, and to convince them that he governs and will judge the world, and that there is a future state of rewards and punishments, and to preach to them a Christ in heaven, at the right hand of God, in an unseen world—shall then meet their people in the most immediate sensible presence of this great God, Savior, and Judge, appearing in the most plain, visible, and open manner, with great glory, with all his holy angels, before them and the whole world. They shall not meet them to hear about an absent Christ, an unseen Lord, and future Judge; but to appear before that Judge—being set together in the presence of that supreme Lord—in his immense glory and awful majesty, of whom they have heard so often in their meetings together on earth.

Fourthly: the meeting at the last day, of ministers and the people that have been under their care, will not be attended by anyone with a careless, heedless heart. With such a heart are their meetings often attended in this world by many persons, having little regard to him whom they pretend unitedly to adore in the solemn duties of his public worship, taking little heed to their own thoughts or frame of their minds, not attending to the business they are engaged in, or considering the end for which they are come together. But at that great day there will not be one careless heart: no sleeping, no wandering of mind from the great concern of the meeting, no inattentiveness to the business of the day, no regardlessness of the presence they are in or of those great things which they shall hear from Christ, or that they formerly heard from him, and of him, by their ministers in their state of trial, or which they shall now hear their ministers declaring concerning them before their Judge.

Having observed these things, concerning the manner and circumstances of this future meeting, before the tribunal of Christ at the day of judgment, I now proceed,

II. To observe to what *purposes* they shall then meet.

1. *To give an account, before the great Judge, of their behavior one to another, in the relation they bore to each other in this world.* Ministers are sent forth by Christ to their people on his business. They are his servants and messengers; and, when they have finished their service, they must return to their master to give him an account of what they have done, and of the entertainment they have had in performing their ministry. Thus we find, in Luke 14:16–21, that when the servant who was sent forth to call the guests to the great supper, had finished his appointed service, he returned to his master, and gave him an account of what he had done, and of the entertainment he had received. And when the master, being angry, sent his servant to others, he returns again and gives his master an account of his conduct and success. So we read, in Heb. 13:17, of ministers or rulers in the house of God, that "they watch for souls, as those that must give account." And we see by the aforementioned Luke 14, that ministers must give an account to their master, not only of their own behavior in the discharge of their office, but also of their people's reception of them, and of the treatment they have met with among them.

Faithful ministers will then give an account with joy, concerning those who have received them well, and made a good improvement of their ministry; and these will be given them, at that day, as their crown of rejoicing. And, at the same time, they will give an account of the ill treatment of such as have not well received them and their messages from Christ. They will meet these, not as they used to do in this world, to counsel and warn them, but to bear witness against them, as their judges and assessors with Christ, to condemn them. And, on the other hand, the people will at that day rise up in judgment against wicked and unfaithful ministers, who have sought their own temporal interest more than the good of the souls of their flock.

2. *At that time ministers, and the people who have been under their care, shall meet together before Christ, that he may judge between them, as to any controversies which have subsisted between them in this world.* It often comes to pass in this evil world, that great differences and controversies arise between ministers and the people under their pastoral care. Though they are under the greatest obligations to live in peace, above persons in almost any relation whatever, and although contests and dissensions between persons so related are the most unhappy and terrible in their consequences on many accounts of any sort of contentions, yet how frequent have such contentions been! Sometimes a people contest with their ministers about their doctrine, sometimes about their administrations and conduct, and sometimes about their maintenance. Sometimes such contests continue a long time, and sometimes they are decided in this world, according to the prevailing interest of one party or the other, rather than by the Word of God, and the reason of things. And sometimes such controversies never have any proper determination in this world.

But at the day of judgment there will be a full, perfect, and everlasting decision of them. The infallible Judge, the infinite fountain of light, truth, and justice, will judge between the contending parties, and will declare what is the truth, who is in the right, and what is agreeable to his mind and will. And in order hereto, the parties must stand together before him at the last day, which will be the great day of finishing and determining all controversies, rectifying all mistakes, and abolishing all unrighteous judgments, errors, and confusions, which have before subsisted in the world of mankind.

3. *Ministers, and the people that have been under their care, must meet together at that time to receive an eternal sentence and retribution from the Judge, in the presence of each other, according to their behavior in the relation they stood in one to another in the present state.* The Judge will not only declare justice, but he will do justice between ministers and their people. He will declare what is right between them, approving him that has been just and faithful, and condemning the unjust. Perfect truth and equity shall take place in the sentence which he passes, in the rewards he bestows, and the punishments

which he inflicts. There shall be a glorious reward to faithful ministers, to those who have been successful. Dan. 12:3, "And they that be wise shall shine as the brightness of the firmament, and they that turn many to righteousness, as the stars forever and ever:" and also to those who have been faithful, and yet not successful, Isa. 49:4, "Then I said, I have labored in vain, I have spent my strength for nought; yet surely my judgment is with the Lord, and my reward with my God." And those who have well received and entertained them shall be gloriously rewarded, Mat. 10:40, 41:

> He that receiveth you, receiveth me; and he that receiveth me, receiveth him that sent me. He that receiveth a prophet in the name of a prophet, shall receive a prophet's reward, and he that receiveth a righteous man, in the name of a righteous man, shall receive a righteous man's reward.

Such people, and their faithful ministers, shall be each other's crown of rejoicing, 1 Thes. 2:19, 20,

> For what is our hope, or joy, or crown of rejoicing? Are not even ye in the presence of our Lord Jesus Christ at his coming? For ye are our glory and joy.

And in the text, "We are your rejoicing, as ye also are ours, in the day of the Lord Jesus." But they that evil entreat Christ's faithful ministers, especially in that wherein they are faithful, shall be severely punished; Mat. 10:14, 15,

> And whosoever shall not receive you, nor hear your words, when ye depart out of that house or city, shake off the dust of your feet. Verily I say unto you, it shall be more tolerable for the sinners of Sodom and Gomorrah, in the day of judgment, than for that city.

Deu. 33:8–11,

> And of Levi he said, "Let thy Thummin and thy Urim be with thy holy one. They shall teach Jacob thy judgments, and Israel thy law. Bless, Lord, his substance, and accept the work of his hands; smite through the loins of them that rise against him, and of them that hate him, that they rise not again."

On the other hand, those ministers who are found to have been unfaithful, shall have a most terrible punishment. (See Eze. 33:6; Mat. 23:1–33.)

Thus justice shall be administered at the great day to ministers and their people: and to that end they shall meet together, that they may not only receive justice to themselves, but see justice done to the other party. For this is the end of that great day, to reveal or declare the righteous judgment of God; Rom. 2:5. Ministers shall have justice done them, and they shall see justice done to their people. And the people shall receive justice themselves from their Judge, and shall see justice done to their minister.

And so all things will be adjusted and settled forever between them: everyone being sentenced and recompensed according to his works, either in receiving and wearing a crown of eternal joy and glory, or in suffering everlasting shame and pain.

III. I come now to the next thing proposed, viz. to give some *reasons* why we may suppose God has so ordered it, that ministers, and the people that have been under their care, shall meet together at the day of judgment, in such a manner and for such purposes.

There are two things which I would now observe.

1. *The mutual concerns of ministers and their people are of the greatest importance.* The Scripture declares that God will bring every work into judgment, with every secret thing, whether it be good or whether it be evil. It is fit that all the concerns and all the behavior of mankind, both public and private, should be brought at last before God's tribunal, and finally determined by an infallible judge. But it is especially requisite that it should be thus, as to affairs of very great importance.

Now the mutual concerns of a Christian minister and his church and congregation, are of the vastest importance: in many respects, of much greater moment than the temporal concerns of the greatest earthly monarchs, and their kingdoms or empires. It is of vast consequence how ministers discharge their office, and conduct themselves towards their people in the work of the ministry, and in affairs appertaining to it. It is also a matter of vast importance, how a people receive and entertain a faithful minister of Christ, and what improvement they make of his ministry. These things have a more immediate and direct respect to the great and last end for which man was made, and the eternal welfare of mankind, than any of the temporal concerns of men, whether private or public. And therefore it is especially fit that these affairs should be brought into judgment, and openly determined and settled, in truth and righteousness, and that to this end, ministers and their people should meet together before the omniscient and infallible Judge.

2. *The mutual concerns of ministers and their people have a special relation to the main things appertaining to the day of judgment.* They have a special relation to that great and divine person who will then appear as Judge. Ministers are his messengers, sent forth by him, and in their office and administrations among their people, represent his person, stand in his stead, as those that are sent to declare his mind, to do his work, and to speak and act in his name. And therefore it is especially fit that they

should return to him to give an account of their work and success. The king is judge of all his subjects, they are all accountable to him. But it is more especially requisite that the king's ministers, who are especially entrusted with the administrations of his kingdom, and who are sent forth on some special negotiation, should return to him, to give an account of themselves, and their discharge of their trust, and the reception they have met with.

Ministers are not only messengers of the person who at the last day will appear as Judge, but the errand they are sent upon, and the affairs they have committed to them as his ministers, most immediately concern his honor, and the interest of his kingdom. The work they are sent upon is to promote the designs of his administration and government, therefore their business with their people has a near relation to the day of judgment. For the great end of that day is completely to settle and establish the affairs of his kingdom, to adjust all things that pertain to it, that everything that is opposite to the interests of his kingdom may be removed, and that everything which contributes to the completeness and glory of it may be perfected and confirmed, that this great King may receive his due honor and glory.

Again, the mutual concerns of ministers and their people have a direct relation to the concerns of the day of judgment, as the business of ministers with their people is to promote the eternal salvation of the souls of men, and their escape from eternal damnation. The day of judgment is the day appointed for that end, openly to decide and settle men's eternal state, to fix some in a state of eternal salvation, and to bring their salvation to its utmost consummation, and to fix others in a state of everlasting damnation and most perfect misery. The mutual concerns of ministers and people have a most direct relation to the day of judgment, as the very design of the work of the ministry is the people's preparation for that day. Ministers are sent to warn them of the approach of that day, to forewarn them of the dreadful sentence then to be pronounced on the wicked, and declare to them the blessed sentence then to be pronounced on the righteous, and to use means with them that they may escape the wrath which is then to come on the ungodly, and obtain the reward then to be bestowed on the saints.

And as the mutual concerns of ministers and their people have so near and direct a relation to that day, it is especially fit that those concerns should there settled and issued, and that in order to this, ministers and their people should meet and appear together before the great Judge at that day.

Application

The improvement I would make of the subject is to lead the people here present, who have been under my pastoral care, to some reflections, and give them some advice suitable to our present circumstances, relating to what has been lately done in order to our being separated, but expecting to meet each other before the great tribunal at the day of judgment.

The deep and serious consideration of our future most solemn meeting, is certainly most suitable at such a time as this. There having so lately been that done, which, in all probability, will (as to the relation we have heretofore stood in) be followed with an everlasting separation.

How often have we met together in the house of God in this relation! How often have I spoke to you, instructed, counseled, warned, directed, and fed you, and administered ordinances among you, as the people which were committed to my care, and of whose precious souls I had the charge! But in all probability this never will be again.

The prophet Jeremiah, chap. 25:3, puts the people in mind how long he had labored among them in the work of the ministry:

> From the thirteenth year of Josiah, the son of Amon, king of Judah, even unto this day (that is, the three and twentieth year), the word of the Lord came unto me, and I have spoken unto you, rising early and speaking.

I am not about to compare myself with the prophet Jeremiah, but in this respect I can say, as he did that "I have spoken the Word of God to you, unto the three and twentieth year, rising early and speaking." It was three and twenty years, the 15th day of last February, since I have labored in the work of the ministry, in the relation of a pastor to this church and congregation. And though my strength has been weakness, having always labored under great infirmity of body, besides my insufficiency for so great a charge in other respects, yet I have not spared my feeble strength, but have exerted it for the good of your souls. I can appeal to you, as the apostle does to his hearers, Gal. 4:13, "Ye know how through infirmity of the flesh, I preached the gospel unto you." I have spent the prime of my life and strength in labors for your eternal welfare. You are my witnesses that what strength I have had, I have not neglected in idleness, nor laid out in prosecuting worldly schemes, and managing temporal affairs, for the advancement of my outward estate, and aggrandizing myself and family. But [I] have given myself to the work of the ministry, laboring in it night and day, rising early and applying myself to this great business to which Christ appointed me. I have found the work of the ministry among you to be a great work indeed, a work of exceeding care, labor and difficulty. Many have been the heavy burdens that I have borne in it, to which my strength has been very unequal. God called me to bear these burdens; and I bless his name that he has so supported me as to keep me from sinking under them, and that his power herein has been manifested in my weakness. So that although I have often been troubled on every side, yet I have not been distressed; perplexed, but not in despair; cast down, but not destroyed.

But now I have reason to think my work is finished which I had to do as your minister: you have publicly rejected me, and my opportunities cease.

How highly therefore does it now become us to consider of that time when we must meet one another before the chief Shepherd! When I must give an account of my stewardship, of the service I have done for, and the reception and treatment I have had among the people to whom he sent me. And you must give an account of your own conduct towards me, and the improvement you have made of these three and twenty years of my ministry. For then both you and I must appear together, and we both must give an account, in order to an infallible, righteous and eternal sentence to be passed upon us, by him who will judge us with respect to all that we have said or done in our meeting here, and all our conduct one towards another in the house of God and elsewhere. [He] will try our hearts, and manifest our thoughts, and the principles and frames of our minds. He will judge us with respect to all the controversies which have subsisted between us, with the strictest impartiality, and will examine our treatment of each other in those controversies.

There is nothing covered that shall not be revealed, nor hid which shall not be known. All will be examined in the searching, penetrating light of God's omniscience and glory, and by him whose eyes are as a flame of fire. Truth and right shall be made plainly to appear, being stripped of every veil. And all error, falsehood, unrighteousness, and injury shall be laid open, stripped of every disguise. Every specious pretense, every cavil, and all false reasoning shall vanish in a moment, as not being able to bear the light of that day. And then our hearts will be turned inside out, and the secrets of them will be made more plainly to appear than our outward actions do now. Then it shall appear what the ends are which we have aimed at, what have been the governing principles which we have acted from, and what have been the dispositions we have exercised in our ecclesiastical disputes and contests. Then it will appear whether I acted uprightly, and from a truly conscientious, careful regard to my duty to my great Lord and Master, in some former ecclesiastical controversies, which have been attended with exceeding unhappy circumstances and consequences. It will appear whether there was any just cause for the resentment which was manifested on those occasions. And then our late grand controversy, concerning the qualifications necessary for admission to the privileges of members, in complete standing, in the visible church of Christ, will be examined and judged in all its parts and circumstances, and the whole set forth in a clear, certain, and perfect light.

Then it will appear whether the doctrine which I have preached and published concerning this matter be Christ's own doctrine, whether he will not own it as one of the precious truths which have proceeded from his own mouth, and vindicate and honor as such before the whole universe. Then it will appear what is meant by "the man that comes without the wedding garment;" for that is the day spoken of, Mat. 22:13, wherein such a one shall be "bound hand and foot, and cast into outer darkness, where shall be weeping and gnashing of teeth." And then it will appear whether, in declaring this doctrine, and acting agreeable to it, and in my general conduct in the affair, I have been influenced from any regard to my own temporal interest, or honor, or desire to appear wiser than others, or have acted from any sinister, secular views whatsoever, and whether what I have done has not been from a careful, strict, and tender regard to the will of my Lord and Master, and because I dare not offend him, being satisfied what his will was, after a long, diligent, impartial, and prayerful inquiry. Then it will be seen whether I had this constantly in view and prospect, to engage me to great solicitude not rashly to determine the question, that such a determination would not be for my temporal interest, but every way against it, bringing a long series of extreme difficulties, and plunging me into an abyss of trouble and sorrow. And then it will appear whether my people have done their duty to their pastor with respect to this matter; whether they have shown a right temper and spirit on this occasion; whether they have done me justice in hearing, attending to and considering what I had to say in evidence of what I believed and taught as part of the counsel of God; whether I have been treated with that impartiality, candor, and regard which the just Judge esteemed due; and whether, in the many steps which have been taken, and the many things that have been said and done in the course of this controversy, righteousness, and charity, and Christian decorum have been maintained; or, if otherwise, to how great a degree these things have been violated. Then every step of the conduct of each of us in this affair, from first to last, and the spirit we have exercised in all, shall be examined and manifested, and our own consciences shall speak plain and loud, and each of us shall be convinced, and the world shall know; and never shall there be any more mistake, misrepresentation, or misapprehension of the affair to eternity.

This controversy is now probably brought to an issue between you and me as to this world. It has issued in the event of the week before last, but it must have another decision at that great day, which certainly will come, when you and I shall meet together before the great judgment seat. Therefore I leave it to that time, and shall say no more about it at present.

But I would now proceed to address myself particularly to several sorts of persons.

1. To those who are *professors* of godliness amongst us.

I would now call you to a serious consideration of that great day wherein you must meet him who has heretofore been your pastor, before the Judge whose eyes are as a flame of fire.

I have endeavored, according to my best ability, to search the Word of God, with regard to the distinguishing notes of true piety, those by which persons might best discover their state, and most surely and clearly judge of themselves. And these rules and marks I have from time to time applied to you, in the preaching of the Word to the utmost of my skill, and in the most plain and search manner that I have been able, in order to the detecting the deceived hypocrite, and establishing the hopes and comforts of the sincere. And yet it is to be feared, that after all that I have done, I now leave some of you in a deceived, deluded state. For it is not to be supposed that among several hundred professors, none are deceived.

Henceforward I am like to have no more opportunity to take the care and charge of your souls, to examine and search them. But still I entreat you to remember and consider the rules which I have often laid down to you during my ministry, with a solemn regard to the future day when you and I must meet together before our Judge, when the uses of examination you have heard from me must be rehearsed again before you, and those rules of trial must be tried, and it will appear whether they have been good or not. It will also appear whether you have impartially heard them, and tried yourselves by them. The Judge himself, who is infallible, will try both you and me. And after this none will be deceived concerning the state of their souls.

I have often put you in mind, that whatever your pretenses to experiences, discoveries, comforts, and joys have been, at that day everyone will be judged according to his works, and then you will find it so. May you have a minister of greater knowledge of the Word of God, and better acquaintance with soul cases, and of greater skill in applying himself to souls, whose discourses may be more searching and convincing, that such of you as have held fast [to] deceit under my preaching, may have your eyes opened by his: that you may be undeceived before that great day.

What means and helps for instruction and self-examination you may hereafter have is uncertain. But one thing is certain: that the time is short—your opportunity for rectifying mistakes in so important a concern will soon come to an end. We live in a world of great changes. There is now a great change come to pass. You have withdrawn yourselves from my ministry, under which you have continued for so many years. But the time is coming, and will soon come, when you will pass out of time into eternity, and so will pass from under all means of grace whatsoever.

The greater part of you who are professors of godliness have (to use the phrase of the apostle) "acknowledged me, in part:" you have heretofore acknowledged me to be your spiritual father, the instrument of the greatest good to you that can be obtained by any of the children of men. Consider of that day when you and I shall meet before our Judge, when it shall be examined whether you have had from me the treatment which is due to spiritual children, and whether you have treated me as you ought to have treated a spiritual father.

As the relation of a natural parent brings great obligations on children in the sight of God, so much more, in many respects, does the relation of a spiritual father bring great obligations on such of whose conversation and eternal salvation they suppose God has made them the instruments, 1 Cor. 4:15, "For though you have ten thousand instructors in Christ, yet have ye not many fathers: for in Christ Jesus, I have begotten you through the gospel."

2. To those in a *Christless, graceless* condition.

Now I am taking my leave of this people, I would apply myself to such among them as I leave in a Christless, graceless condition, and would call on such seriously to consider of that solemn day when they and I must meet before the Judge of the world.

My parting with you is, in some respects, in a peculiar manner a melancholy parting, inasmuch as I leave you in most melancholy circumstances, because I leave you in the gall of bitterness and bond of iniquity, having the wrath of God abiding on you, and remaining under condemnation to everlasting misery and destruction. Seeing I must leave you, it would have been a comfortable and happy circumstance of our parting, if I had left you in Christ, safe and blessed in that sure refuge and glorious rest of the saints. But it is otherwise. I leave you far off, aliens and strangers, wretched subjects and captives of sin and Satan, and prisoners of vindictive justice: without Christ, and without God in the world.

Your consciences bear me witness that while I had opportunity, I have not ceased to warn you, and set before you your danger. I have studied to represent the misery and necessity of your circumstances in the clearest manner possible. I have tried all ways that I could think of tending to awaken your consciences, and make you sensible of the necessity of your improving your time, and being speedy in flying from the wrath to come, and thorough in the use of means for your escape and safety. I have diligently endeavored to find out and use the most powerful motives to persuade you to take care for your own welfare and salvation. I have not only endeavored to awaken you, that you might be moved with fear, but I have used my utmost endeavors to win you: I have sought out acceptable words, that if possible I might prevail upon you to forsake sin, and turn to God, and accept of Christ as your Savior and Lord. I have spent my strength very much in these things. But yet, with regard to you whom I am addressing, I have not been successful, but have this day reason to complain in those words, Jer. 6:29: "The bellows are burnt, the lead is consumed of the fire, the founder melteth in vain, for the wicked are not plucked away." It is to be feared that all my labors, as to many of you, have served no other purpose but to harden you, and that the word which I have preached, instead of being a savor of life unto life, has been a savor of death unto death. Though I shall not have any account to give for the future of such as have openly and resolutely renounced my ministry, as of a trust committed to me, yet remember you must give account for yourselves, of your care of your own souls, and your improvement of all means past and future, through your whole lives. God only knows what will become of your poor perishing souls, what means you may hereafter enjoy, or what disadvantages and temptations you may be under. May God in his mercy grant that however all past means have been unsuccessful, you may have future means which may have a new effect, and that the Word of God, as it shall be hereafter dispensed to you, may prove as the fire and the hammer that breaketh the rock in pieces. However, let me now at parting exhort and beseech you not wholly to forget the warnings you have had while under my ministry. When you and I shall meet at the day of judgment, then you will remember them. The sight of me, your former minister, on that occasion, will soon revive them in your memory; and that in a very affecting manner. O do not let that be the first time that they are so revived.

You and I are now parting one from another as to this world. Let us labor that we may not be parted after our meeting at the last day. If I have been your faithful pastor (which will that day appear whether I have or no), then I shall be acquitted, and shall ascend with Christ. O do your part that in such a case, you may not be forced eternally to part from me, and all that have been faithful in Christ Jesus. *This* is a sorrowful parting, but *that* would be a more sorrowful. *This,* you may perhaps bear without being much affected with it, if you are not glad of it, but such a parting in *that* day will most deeply, sensibly, and dreadfully affect you.

3. I would address myself to those who are under some *awakenings.*

Blessed be God that there are some such, and that (although I have reason to fear I leave multitudes in this large congregation in a Christless state) yet I do not leave them all in total stupidity and carelessness about their souls. Some of you that I have reason to hope are under some awakenings, have acquainted me with your circumstances, which has a tendency to cause me, now I am leaving you, to take my leave with peculiar concern for you. What will be the issue of your present exercise of mind, I know not, but it will be known at that day, when you and I shall meet before the judgment seat of Christ. Therefore now be much in consideration of that day.

Now I am parting with this flock, I would once more press upon you the counsels I have heretofore given, to take heed of slightly so great a concern, to be thorough and in good earnest in the affair, and to beware of backsliding, to hold on and hold out to the end. And cry mightily to God, that these great changes which pass over this church and congregation do not prove your overthrow. There is great temptation in them, and the devil will undoubtedly seek to make his advantage of them, if possible to cause your present convictions and endeavors to be abortive. You had need to double your diligence, and watch and pray, lest you be overcome by temptation.

Whoever may hereafter stand related to you as your spiritual guide, my desire and prayer is that the great Shepherd of the sheep would have a special respect to you, and be your guide (for there is none teacheth like him), and that he who is the infinite fountain of light, would "open your eyes, and turn you from darkness unto light, and from the power of Satan unto God; that you may receive forgiveness of sins, and inheritance among them that are sanctified, through faith that is in Christ;" that so in that great day, when I shall meet you again before your Judge and mine, we may meet in joyful and glorious circumstances, never to be separated any more.

4. I would apply myself to the *young people* of the congregation.

Since I have been settled in the work of the ministry in this place, I have ever had a peculiar concern for the souls of the young people, and a desire that religion might flourish among them; and have especially exerted myself in order to it, because I knew the special opportunity they had beyond others, and that ordinarily those for whom God intended mercy, were brought to fear and love him in their youth. And it has ever appeared to me a peculiarly amiable thing, to see young people walking in the ways of virtue and Christian piety, having their hearts purified and sweetened with a principle of divine love. How exceeding beautiful, and conducive to the adorning and happiness of the town, if the young people could be persuaded, when they meet together, to converse as Christians and as the children of God, avoiding impurity, levity and extravagance, keeping strictly to rules of virtue and conversing together of the things of God, and Christ, and heaven! This is what I have longed for, and it has been exceeding grievous to me when I have heard of vice, vanity and disorder among our youth. And so far as I know my own heart, it was from hence that I formerly led this church to some measures, for the suppressing vice among our young people, which gave so great offense, and by which I became so obnoxious. I have sought the good, and not the hurt of our young people. I have desired their truest honor and happiness, and not their reproach: knowing that true virtue and religion tended not only to the glory and felicity of young people in another world, but their greatest peace and prosperity, and highest dignity and honor in this world, and above all things to sweeten, and render pleasant and delightful, even the days of youth. But whether I have loved you, and sought your good more or less, now committing your souls to him who once committed the pastoral care of them to me—nothing remains, but only (as I am now taking my leave of you) earnestly to beseech you, from love to yourselves, if you have none to me, not to despise and forget the warnings and counsels I have so often given you. Remember the day when you and I must meet again before the great Judge of quick and dead, when it will appear whether the things I have taught you were true, whether the counsels I have given you were good, and whether I truly sought your welfare, and whether you have well improved my endeavors. I have, from time to time, earnestly warned you against *frolicking* (as it is called), and some other liberties commonly taken by young people in the land. And whatever some may say in justification of such liberties and customs, and may laugh at warnings against them, I now leave you my parting testimony against such things, not doubting but God will approve and confirm it in that day when we shall meet before him.

5. I would apply myself to the *children* of the congregation, the lambs of this flock, who have been so long under my care.

I have just now said that I have had a peculiar concern for the young people, and in so saying I did not intend to exclude you. You are in youth, and in the most early youth. Therefore I have been sensible that if those that were young had a precious opportunity for their souls' good, you who are very young had, in many respects, a peculiarly precious opportunity. And accordingly I have not neglected you. I have endeavored to do the part of a faithful shepherd, in feeding the lambs as well as the sheep. Christ did once commit the care of your souls to me as your minister; and you know, dear children, how I have instructed you, and warned you from time to time. You know how I have often called you together for that end, and some of you, sometimes, have seemed to be affected with what I have said to you. But I am afraid it has had no saving effect as to many of you, but that you remain still in an unconverted condition, without any real saving work wrought in your souls, convincing you thoroughly of your sin and misery, causing you to see the great evil of sin, and to mourn for it, and hate it above all things, and giving you a sense of the excellency of the Lord Jesus Christ, bringing you with all your hearts to cleave to him as your Savior, weaning your hearts from the world, and causing you to love God above all, and to delight in holiness more than in all the pleasant things of this earth. And I must now leave you in a miserable condition, having no interest in Christ, and so under the awful displeasure and anger of God, and in danger of going down to the pit of eternal misery. Now I must bid you farewell. I must leave you in the hands of God. I can do no more for you than to pray for you. Only I desire you not to forget, but often think of the counsels and warnings I have given you, and the endeavors I have used, that your souls might be saved from everlasting destruction. Dear children, I leave you in an evil world, that is full of snares and temptations. God only knows what will become of you. This the Scripture has told us: that there are but few saved, and we have abundant confirmation of it from what we see. This we see, that children die as well as others. Multitudes die before they grow up, and of those that grow up, comparatively few ever give good evidence of saving conversion to God. I pray God to pity you, and take care of you, and provide for you the best means for the good of your souls, and that God himself would undertake for you to be your heavenly Father, and the mighty Redeemer of your immortal souls. Do not neglect to pray for yourselves. Take heed you be not of the number of those who cast off fear, and restrain prayer before God. Constantly pray to God in secret, and often remember that great day when you must appear before the judgment seat of Christ, and meet your minister there, who has so often counseled and warned you.